Emily Brontë's
WUTHERING
HEIGHTS

Bloom's
NOTES

A Contemporary
Literary Views Book

Edited and with an Introduction by
HAROLD BLOOM

3 5 7 9 8 6 4

Cover illustration: Photofest

Library of Congress Cataloging-in-Publication Data

Emily Brontë's Wuthering Heights / edited and with an introduction by Harold Bloom.
p.   cm. — (Bloom's Notes)
Includes bibliographical references and index.
ISBN 0-7910-3673-1
1. Brontë, Emily, 1818–1848. Wuthering Heights. 2. Yorkshire (England) in literature. I. Bloom, Harold. II. Series: Bloom, Harold. Bloom's Notes.
PR4172.W73E45 1996
823'.8—dc20
95-23728
CIP

Chelsea House Publishers
1974 Sproul Road, Suite 400
P.O. Box 914
Broomall, PA 19008-0914

Contents

User's Guide   4

Introduction   5

Biography of Emily Brontë   8

Thematic and Structural Analysis   10

List of Characters   22

Critical Views   25

Books by Emily Brontë   73

Works about Emily Brontë and *Wuthering Heights*   75

Index of Themes and Ideas   78

User's Guide

This volume is designed to present biographical, critical, and bibliographical information on Emily Brontë and *Wuthering Heights*. Following Harold Bloom's introduction, there appears a detailed biography of the author, discussing the major events in her life and her important literary works. Then follows a thematic and structural analysis of the work, in which significant themes, patterns, and motifs are traced. An annotated list of characters supplies brief information on the chief characters in the work.

A selection of critical extracts, derived from previously published material by leading critics, then follows. The extracts consist of statements by the author on her work, early reviews of the work, and later evaluations down to the present day. The items are arranged chronologically by date of first publication. A bibliography of Brontë's writings (including a complete listing of all books she wrote, cowrote, edited, and translated), a list of additional books and articles on her and on *Wuthering Heights,* and an index of themes and ideas conclude the volume.

Harold Bloom is Sterling Professor of the Humanities at Yale University and Henry W. and Albert A. Berg Professor of English at the New York University Graduate School. He is the author of twenty books and the editor of more than thirty anthologies of literature and literary criticism.

Professor Bloom's works include *Shelley's Mythmaking* (1959), *The Visionary Company* (1961), *Blake's Apocalypse* (1963), *Yeats* (1970), *A Map of Misreading* (1975), *Kabbalah and Criticism* (1975), and *Agon: Towards a Theory of Revisionism* (1982). *The Anxiety of Influence* (1973) sets forth Professor Bloom's provocative theory of the literary relationships between the great writers and their predecessors. His most recent books are *The American Religion* (1992) and *The Western Canon* (1994).

Professor Bloom earned his Ph.D. from Yale University in 1955 and has served on the Yale faculty since then. He is a 1985 MacArthur Foundation Award recipient and served as the Charles Eliot Norton Professor of Poetry at Harvard University in 1987–88. He is currently the editor of the Chelsea House series Major Literary Characters and Modern Critical Views, and other Chelsea House series in literary criticism.

Introduction

HAROLD BLOOM

Wuthering Heights is one of those canonical works or classics that reward readers at every level of literary sophistication. I suspect that this has to do with the strangeness or originality that Emily Brontë's idiosyncratic "northern romance" possesses in such abundance. *Wuthering Heights* is like nothing else in the language, though the closest work to it, the sister-book as it were, is Charlotte Brontë's *Jane Eyre.* Yet Charlotte rejected the affinity, and regarded Heathcliff as "a mere demon." Heathcliff is much more than that; as a negative hero or hero-villain he has the sublimity of Captain Ahab in Herman Melville's *Moby-Dick,* and something even of the darkened splendor of Satan in Milton's *Paradise Lost.* Emily Brontë's implicit model for Heathcliff was the long poem *Manfred,* a self-portrait by Lord Byron in which the Romantic poet allows himself to absorb aspects of Milton's Satan. Despite Heathcliff's sadism, he is however Satanic primarily in his wounded pride. His obsessive love for Catherine Earnshaw is the only principle of his being. This passion is so monumental and so destructive, of everyone, that it seems inadequate and imprecise to call it "love." To define the mutual attachment between Heathcliff and the first Catherine is a difficult enterprise, but is essential to understanding *Wuthering Heights.*

One hesitates to term the relationship between Heathcliff and Catherine even potentially sexual, since sexual love unites in act, but not in essence, and Catherine is capable of saying: "I *am* Heathcliff." As you reread *Wuthering Heights,* you come to see that there are two orders of reality in the novel, with only tenuous connectors between them. One is *both* social and natural, while the other is neither, being the realm of dreams, ghosts, visions, and (most importantly) the transcendental yearnings of all our childhoods. That second realm is neither psychological nor spiritual; Emily Brontë was neither a moral psychologist nor a Christian, though she was a clergyman's daughter. Doomed, like all her siblings, to an early death from tuberculosis, she learned to dwell in her deepest self, which is the theater where the drama of *Wuthering Heights* is performed. The two oldest Brontë sisters, Maria and Elizabeth, died in 1825, aged eleven and ten. Charlotte, the family survivor, died at thirty-eight, after mourning the deaths of Emily, aged thirty, her brother Branwell, at thirty-one, and Anne, at twenty-nine. *Wuthering Heights,* completed when Emily Brontë was twenty-eight, gives us a world in which everyone marries young because they seem to know that they will not live very long. Catherine Earnshaw dies at eighteen, Hindley at twenty-seven, Isabella at thirty-one, Linton Heathcliff at seventeen, Edgar at thirty-nine, and Heathcliff, probably, at about thirty-seven. At the end of the book, Hareton and the second Catherine are twenty-four and eighteen, respectively, when they happily marry. While the urgency of all this has both its societal and its natural aspects, the larger suggestion is a kind of doom-eagerness, impatient alike of society and of nature.

Moral judgments, whether of her own day or of ours, become rapidly irrelevant in the world of Emily Brontë's one novel. Though the book portrays both social and natural energies, these are dwarfed by the preternatural energies of Heathcliff and of the antithetical side of the first Catherine. Where daemonic energy so far exceeds ours, then daemonic suffering will also be present, perhaps also in excess of our own. But such suffering is foreign to us; Emily Brontë accepts the aesthetic risk of endowing Heathcliff with very little pathos recognizable by us. We wonder at his terrible sufferings, as he slowly dies from lack of sleep and lack of food, but we do not *feel* his agony, because he has become even more distant from us. We are partly moved by the first Catherine's death, since both society and nature are involved in her decline, but partly we stand away from participation, because Catherine is also very much of the realm she shares with Heathcliff. For the last half-year of his life, she is a ghostly presence, but one not much different from what she has been for him before.

The first Catherine is the only bridge we have to the mystery of Heathcliff, since only Catherine lives both in the realistic and occult worlds that confront one another in *Wuthering Heights.* E. M. Forster, in his *Aspects of the Novel* (1927), remarked that: "*Wuthering Heights* has no mythology beyond what these two characters provide: no great book is more cut off from the universals of Heaven and Hell." That seems true to me, and it makes Emily Brontë's great narrative an anomaly; it is of no clear genre. But it gives us, finally, something larger and stronger even than Heathcliff, something that I would want to call more than the personal vision of Emily Brontë. The transcendental element in the book cannot be assigned any traditional name, but its force and its persuasiveness cannot be evaded or ignored. Emily Brontë prophesied no religion except that of the "God within my breast," and *Wuthering Heights* profoundly implies that Heathcliff and Catherine reunite in a here-and-now that yet is not our present world, or any world to come for most among us. ❖

Biography of Emily Brontë

Emily Jane Brontë was born on July 30, 1818, at Thornton, near Bradford, Yorkshire. She was the fifth child and fourth daughter of the Reverend Patrick Brontë and Maria Branwell (Patrick later changed his name to Branwell Brontë). Emily's sisters Charlotte (1816–1855) and Anne (1820–1849) were also writers, as was her brother Branwell (1817–1848) to a more limited extent. In 1820 the family moved to Haworth, where Branwell senior obtained a curacy. The next year Emily's mother died; her sister Elizabeth kept house for the family until she herself died in 1842. Emily briefly attended the Clergy Daughters' School at Cowan Bridge in 1824–25 but thereafter was largely educated at home. Beginning in 1826 the Brontë children, fascinated by some toy soldiers their father had brought home, conceived of an imaginary African kingdom called Angria; later Emily and Anne invented a separate kingdom in the Pacific called Gondal. They all wrote poems and prose sketches about these kingdoms for the rest of their lives.

For a period in 1835 Emily accompanied Charlotte as a tutor at a school in East Yorkshire, but she was unhappy there and quickly returned to Haworth. In 1837 or 1838 she worked as a governess at Law Hill, near Halifax; a house near this school, High Sunderland Hall, is thought by some scholars to be the chief inspiration for Wuthering Heights. In 1842, as part of a plan to open a school at Haworth, Emily went to the Pensionnat Heger in Brussels with Charlotte to study languages; but, although she was praised for her intellect and especially her mastery of French, her forbidding manner attracted few pupils.

Returning to Haworth late in 1842, Emily devoted herself to the writing of poetry about Gondal. Much of this poetry is full of the same violent, cruel characters that populate *Wuthering Heights*. In the autumn of 1845 Charlotte discovered a notebook containing this poetry; although Emily was at first highly incensed at the discovery, she was gradually persuaded to let Charlotte seek its publication. In 1846 a collection of verse by

Charlotte, Emily, and Anne appeared as *Poems by Currer, Ellis, and Acton Bell* (their respective pseudonyms). Emily wrote only one more poem in her lifetime, for by this time she was at work on her one novel.

Wuthering Heights was written between October 1845 and June 1846 and published in December 1847, again under the pseudonym of Ellis Bell. It was not well received and puzzled most of its readers; many of them regarded it as excessively morbid, violent, and indelicate. In the years since Emily Brontë's death the book has found its readership and a steadily growing reputation. It is now considered one of the master-pieces of nineteenth-century fiction and one of the most original novels in English literature.

It is conjectured that Emily was working on an expanded version of *Wuthering Heights* in the final year or so prior to her death; but this version, if there was one, has not been found. Otherwise, little is known of the final two years of her life. Emily Brontë died of tuberculosis at the age of thirty on December 19, 1848. ❖

Thematic and Structural Analysis

Emily Brontë's *Wuthering Heights* is a love story set in the desolate moorlands of northern England at the end of the eighteenth century. It spans a period of some forty years, following the repercussions of the fiery, doomed love of the novel's protagonists, Cathy and Heathcliff. Passion, both love and hatred, erupt with ferocity in Brontë's Gothic world, yet she simultaneously creates a degree of critical distance from the drama by using a disinterested secondhand narrator. Lockwood, a newcomer from London, records the story in his diary after hearing it from his housekeeper Nelly Dean. Because many of Nelly's characters are living people whom Lockwood meets during the course of his stay, and because daily life interrupts her tale several times—a hiatus of nine months postpones the narration of the final events—Brontë also creates a troubling, distorted sense of time. The present world is haunted not only by past events; the novel is also framed by a pair of unresolved ghostly visitations which leave the two most incredulous characters—Lockwood and Nelly Dean—wondering at the spiritual mysteries of Wuthering Heights.

The novel begins with Lockwood's diary entry from the winter of 1801. As a new tenant of the Thrushcross Grange estate, he pays a visit to his landlord, Mr. Heathcliff. Both the neighboring estate, Wuthering Heights—a grim thick-walled farmhouse—and his host are singularly unwelcoming. Within minutes of his arrival an angry pack of dogs attacks him. Heathcliff and the servant Joseph belatedly and ungraciously save him and Lockwood leaves, disgusted. On a second visit he meets Heathcliff's beautiful but unfriendly widowed daughter-in-law, Catherine, and her sullen, illiterate cousin Hareton Earnshaw. Lockwood offends his hosts by mistaking Catherine for Heathcliff's wife and then for Hareton's wife, and he poses a further inconvenience by finding he must stay overnight: a snowstorm begun during his visit prevents his departure.

His hosts make no effort to accommodate him until the housekeeper, at the beginning of **chapter three,** shows him to a small bedchamber. Lockwood finds the name of Catherine carved on the old-fashioned paneled bed and discovers some old schoolbooks, including a fragment of what proves to be the late Cathy Earnshaw's diary. Her youthful scribblings describe a painful Sunday under the guardianship of her older brother, Hindley. The interminable preaching of Joseph (a servant whom Lockwood himself has met), memorization of Bible passages, Hindley's anger, and her imprisonment in the washroom make up the familiar pattern of her day. In the end she breaks off, deciding to escape to the moors with her playmate Heathcliff.

Lockwood nods off and is plagued by nightmares. He dreams that he hears a tree knocking on the window and that he breaks the glass to tear off the branch. Reaching out into the storm he is grabbed by an ice-cold hand. He sees a child's face outside, and a voice identifying itself as Catherine Linton begs to be let in. When he panics and tries to release the grip by rubbing the spirit's wrist against the broken glass, his terror and the sight of the blood make him yell himself awake. The noise rouses Heathcliff. Horrified to find Lockwood in his dead beloved's bedchamber, he orders him to leave. Lockwood then unwillingly witnesses Heathcliff's desperate anguish. Thinking himself alone, his host throws open the windows and tearfully begs Cathy's ghost to enter.

Heathcliff reappears for breakfast transformed from wretched lover to an angry brutish master, roughly upbraiding Catherine, who lashes back. Lockwood leaves the grim household with renewed disgust. He catches a bad cold on his journey home. For most of the remaining novel (**chapters four through thirty**) he lies in bed listening eagerly to his housekeeper's story of how Wuthering Heights arrived at its present state.

Nelly was a servant at Wuthering Heights when she was little, growing up with the Earnshaw family's children. She begins her story with the arrival of Heathcliff, when Hindley Earnshaw was fourteen and his sister Cathy was six. Their father returned from a trip to London with a mysterious ragged gypsy child, whom the family first greeted with horror. Grudgingly accepted, Heathcliff, as he was called, became the master's favorite and grew to be Cathy's ally and Hindley's hated enemy. Cathy was a willful, spontaneous child, "[h]er spirits . . .

always at high-water mark," constantly in trouble or playing the "little mistress." Heathcliff was stoically hardened and single-minded, in one instance withstanding Hindley's brutal thrashing to blackmail him into giving up his pony.

Cathy's mother dies, Hindley leaves for college, and the increasingly authoritarian master passes away three years later. At his funeral Hindley arrives married to a weak, silly woman. He takes over Wuthering Heights and immediately cuts off Heathcliff's education, forcing him to work as a destitute farm laborer. Cathy also suffers under her cruel brother, but their punishments only make the two friends more reckless and more devoted to each other.

One Sunday evening (here in **chapter six** Nelly's story adroitly picks up where Cathy's diary had left off) Cathy and Heathcliff escape to the moors and sneak up to the neighboring Linton estate, Thrushcross Grange. They see the spoiled children Edgar and Isabella through the window, in the throes of a tantrum. Before they can leave the guard dogs attack; one grabs Cathy's ankle and the two are caught. When they are brought inside, Edgar recognizes Cathy and the family rushes to her aid. Meanwhile dark, ragged Heathcliff is declared "unfit for a decent house" and thrown out, leaving Cathy surrounded by a doting family.

This episode contrasts two distinctive spaces in Brontë's novel. Reversing anticipated associations, she describes the cruel unsheltering moor as a savage earthly paradise where Cathy and Heathcliff are free and equal. But the Lintons' comfortable parlor, "a splendid place carpeted with crimson, and crimson covered chairs and tables," is a site of unhappiness; a wrongheaded, restrictive heaven. When Cathy abandons the moor, her shared world with Heathcliff, the act has Biblical connotations, showing her choice as a fall from innocence.

In **chapter seven** Cathy returns at Christmas; after five weeks at Thrushcross Grange, she has become a dignified young lady dressed in furs and silks. Heathcliff, made acutely aware of their different social stations, confides to Nelly that he envies Edgar's looks and breeding. Cathy is torn between her new and old friends, attempting at a Christmas dinner to play a gay hostess to the Lintons but inwardly suffering when Heathcliff, in anger, throws sauce on Edgar and is banished from the table.

Nelly relates how Heathcliff's cruel mistreatment escalates when Hindley's wife dies after giving birth to a son. The husband's grief drives him to drink and gambling. Nelly cares for the boy, Hareton, and watches the dissipation of the once prominent family. "I could not half tell what an infernal house we had," she remembers. Unchecked, Cathy leads a double life, reckless at home but charming to the Lintons. Her mask drops one afternoon when Edgar comes courting (**chapter eight**) and Cathy, incited by a jealous Heathcliff and unindulgent Nelly, takes out her rage on Hareton. Edgar intervenes and she boxes his ear. Shocked, he tries to leave and Cathy breaks into tears. Despite Nelly's prompting he cannot tear himself away. Their fight leads to an open declaration of love.

The day of crisis continues violently. Hindley comes home drunk, threatens Nelly with a carving knife, and nearly drops Hareton to his death. He showers Heathcliff with more abuse, and Heathcliff vows revenge. That evening an angry but half-repentant Cathy seeks Nelly's advice. She has accepted Edgar's proposal of marriage but feels uneasy. In an important speech in **chapter nine** she explains why the engagement makes her so unhappy. She tells how she had once dreamed she was in heaven, and she had been so miserable and homesick that the angry angels had flung her back to earth, where she awoke on the heath "sobbing for joy." She insists that marrying Edgar would be like going to that heaven; she would be unhappy and grieve for Heathcliff, her second half. She proclaims, "he's more myself than I am! Whatever our souls are made of, his and mine are the same; and Linton's is as different as a moonbeam from lightning, or frost from fire." The speech recalls the imagery of the sixth chapter; of the Linton's house as an unhappy, restrictive heaven. It also presents love, unconventionally for its time, as a passionate union of equals and soul mates.

As Nelly listens she notices that Heathcliff has overheard from an adjoining room but has left before Cathy's admission of love, stung by her assertion that to marry him penniless would degrade her. His departure is discovered at the evening meal. A summer thunderstorm breaks out. Nature, as is often the case in Brontë's world, acts here as an empathetic participant in the crisis of characters who are themselves so closely associated with their surrounding landscape. Cathy, distraught, spends the night looking for Heathcliff. In the morning, drenched and grief ridden, she becomes delirious and falls gravely ill. He does not return, and a long period of convalescence ensues. Nelly passes quickly over the events of the next three years: Cathy's recovery, the death of both Linton parents, Hindley's continued life of debauchery, and Cathy's marriage. Nelly goes to live with her mistress at Thrushcross Grange, regretfully leaving Hareton in the hands of his negligent father.

Here (**chapter ten**) Nelly interrupts her story, leaving Lockwood in a weak, fretful state. Several characters from her narrative come to pay visits, oddly telescoping the passage of time. They include the doctor who had overseen Hareton's birth and Cathy's delirium, and Heathcliff himself. After four irksome weeks Lockwood calls Nelly to finish her story.

Resuming, Nelly skims over the first happy year of Cathy's marriage, when an indulgent Edgar and Isabella humored her every wish. "It was not the thorn bending to the honeysuckles, but the honeysuckles embracing the thorn." Heathcliff soon shatters this peace. He returns one September evening, approaching Nelly in the garden, who at first does not recognize the tall, well-dressed gentleman. Cathy is overwhelmed with joy, but the enraptured reunion of his wife and guest strains Edgar's politeness to its limit. He unwillingly tolerates Heathcliff's continued visits. Much to Nelly's surprise Heathcliff moves in with his old enemy Hindley, who has lost to him at cards and is eager to reclaim his debts. Meanwhile eighteen-year-old Isabella develops a crush on Heathcliff, eventually divulging her secret to Cathy. Cathy contemptuously warns her sister-in-law of the dangers of her friend. Heathcliff, she says, is "an unreclaimed creature, without refinement, without cultivation; an arid wilderness of furze and whinstone. I'd as soon put that little canary into the park on a winter's day, as recommend you to bestow your heart on him!" Isabella insists that Cathy is simply jealous, and stung by this rebuke, Cathy cruelly reveals her sister-in-law's secret to Heathcliff. He admits he detests her "maukish waxen face," so like Edgar's, but learns that she would be her brother's heir were Edgar to die without a son.

In **chapter eleven,** Nelly is troubled by premonitions of a crisis and visits the Heights. Hareton has turned into an angry, violent child taught by Heathcliff to curse his own father. On returning Nelly catches Heathcliff embracing Isabella in the garden. Cathy is called and an argument ensues. Heathcliff accuses Cathy of having treated him "infernally" but claims he seeks no revenge on her, his tyrant, only on those weaker than himself.

When Nelly promptly tells Edgar of what has transpired he tries to throw Heathcliff out of the house. His guest is incredulous: "Cathy, this lamb of yours threatens like a bull. . . . It is in danger of splitting its skull against my knuckles." The confrontation breaks up when Linton leaves for reinforcements and Heathcliff escapes through the back. Cathy, angry at both men, confides to Nelly that she intends to hurt them through her own self-destruction: "I'll try to break their hearts by breaking my own." When Edgar returns Cathy explodes with hysterical rage. Nelly is first convinced that she is acting, but when Cathy overhears this speculation she starts up with renewed fury and locks herself in her room. In the novel her diabolical temper, which sends her husband cowering, is matched only by Heathcliff's pitch of vengeful anger.

Cathy's self-imprisonment and starvation last for three days. When she finally lets Nelly enter (**chapter twelve**) she is weak and half-delirious, though still angry with Edgar. As she slips in and out of lucidity she tells Nelly of her anguish, continually thinking she is back at the Heights and then realizing her prisonlike married state. "Oh, I'm burning!" she cries. "I wish I were out of doors! I wish I were a girl again, half savage and hardy, and free . . . and laughing at injuries, not maddening under them!" Her premonition of losing the invulnerable paradise of her youth has proved all too true. As she opens the windows and calls for Heathcliff, Edgar enters. He is astonished to see her so deteriorated and angrily sends Nelly for the doctor. In the town she hears a rumor that Heathcliff has eloped with Isabella. The news is confirmed the next morning and

Edgar, crushed by his wife's state, quietly disowns his sister without an attempt at pursuit.

The emotional storm of the evening is followed, as after Heathcliff's first departure, by a recuperative lull in the story. Two months of Edgar's attentive care find Cathy well enough to sit but permanently weakened. The reader learns that they are expecting a child. Meanwhile Heathcliff and Isabella return to the Heights. Edgar refuses Isabella's note, who then writes a long letter to Nelly, which is read to Lockwood in **chapter thirteen.** Isabella tells of her husband's appalling cruelty, the primitive conditions of the cold, stony Heights, and its hostile occupants, Hindley, Hareton, and Joseph. She asks Nelly, "Is Mr. Heathcliff a man? If so, is he mad? If not, is he a devil?" Nelly visits, finding Isabella utterly destitute and turned as cruel and vicious as her husband. Before leaving, Heathcliff forces her to promise to help him to see Cathy.

Heathcliff's speech to Nelly relies on a repeated motif from the novel, using imagery from nature to describe a character. Cathy had likened Heathcliff's soul to the arid wilderness of the moors, while Nelly described the Lintons as honeysuckles, cultivated and fragile. Here Heathcliff proclaims of Edgar's meager love: "He might as well plant an oak in a flower-pot and expect it to thrive, as imagine he can restore her to vigor in the soil of his shallow cares!" These metaphors reinforce the contrast of wilderness and cultivation which dominates the novel.

While Edgar nurses Cathy at the Grange, Heathcliff roams the gardens outside. In **chapter fifteen,** Heathcliff spies his chance when Edgar leaves for Sunday church. Cathy is a beautiful, haunting vision of her former self. Heathcliff enters, grasping her in his arms. In the scene that follows both lovers vindictively accuse and forgive each other, realizing that Cathy is going to die. She says she hopes Heathcliff will suffer as he has made her suffer and declares herself eager to escape life, her "shattered prison." In a second impassioned embrace Heathcliff asks Cathy why she had despised him and betrayed her heart. Meanwhile Edgar returns from church and as Cathy, mad with grief, clings to her lover, Nelly tries to force Heathcliff to leave. They are discovered, Cathy falls in a faint, and Edgar forgets everything to attend to her. That evening Cathy gives birth to a baby girl and dies without regaining full consciousness.

While the house is in mourning, Nelly finds Heathcliff in the garden. He is angry and unrepentant. His one prayer is that Cathy will not rest in peace while he is living. "You said I killed you—haunt me then!" he calls to her. Cathy is buried unconventionally in a corner of the churchyard overlooking the heath.

The grief-stricken house is interrupted in **chapter seventeen** by the giddy entrance of Isabella, who has run coatless through a spring snowstorm from the Heights. She sees only Nelly before continuing her escape, telling her of the violent past days at the Heights. Hindley had tried to murder Heathcliff, who had cut his attacker badly and then beaten him. The next morning Isabella had taunted Heathcliff, accusing him of having killed Cathy. In anger he had thrown a knife at her, cutting the side of her head, and she had fled, wildly happy to be free. Isabella leaves and Nelly eventually hears news that she has settled near London and given birth to a weak, sickly child named Linton. Six months later Hindley dies, drunk to the last and so deeply in debt to Heathcliff that his son, Hareton, is forced into dependency on his father's worst enemy.

His death brings the events of the first half of the novel to a close. While this part has a Gothic pitch sustained by its two passionate protagonists, the second half begins in the tone of a fairy tale. In a strange reversal Heathcliff becomes the vengeful, scheming villain, while a new romantic triangle, uncannily reminiscent of his own, unfolds among the second generation. **Chapter eighteen** begins with an idyllic interlude, during which Catherine Linton, Cathy's daughter, grows to adolescence. Nelly is her nursemaid and a saddened Edgar becomes a loving, watchful father. Catherine has both her mother's willful high spirits and her father's tenderness. She lives a secluded life for thirteen years, ignorant of Wuthering Heights or its inhabitants. Then Edgar is called to Isabella's deathbed, leaving Catherine for three weeks. Against Nelly's orders she rides out past the park walls and comes across Wuthering Heights. Nelly finds her happily drinking tea with the housekeeper and a tall, bashful eighteen-year-old Hareton. Catherine ignores Nelly's scolding but leaves after offending a smitten Hareton by mis-taking him for the master and then treating him like a servant. Nelly swears Catherine to secrecy, worried of Edgar's anger.

Isabella dies and Edgar returns with her peevish child. Catherine dotes on her cousin Linton, but when Heathcliff demands his son Edgar has no choice but to comply. The next morning Nelly sneaks Linton to the Heights before Catherine can learn of his fate. The boy is terrified of his father, but Heathcliff, although clearly disgusted with his progeny, tells Nelly he plans to pamper Linton, the heir to Edgar's estate. Reports from the housekeeper confirm Nelly's suspicion that Linton is a selfish, spoiled inmate.

In **chapter twenty-one** Catherine, on her sixteenth birthday, goes for a walk with Nelly and meets Heathcliff and Hareton on the heath. Heathcliff, against Nelly's warnings, cajoles Catherine into visiting Wuthering Heights. Catherine is over-joyed to find her long-lost cousin. Linton, for his part, has grown into a languid self-absorbed teenager, still in delicate health. Heathcliff confides to Nelly that he hopes the two will marry, as he worries that Linton may not live to inherit Edgar's estate. Hareton suffers under Catherine's snubs and leaves angrily when Linton makes fun of his illiteracy. Heathcliff brags that he has reduced Hindley's son to the same destitution as Hindley had once reduced him.

When Edgar learns of Catherine's visit he forbids further trips to the Heights, so Catherine begins a clandestine correspon-dence with her cousin. Nelly soon discovers her secret stash of love letters and forces her to burn them. Several months later Catherine, walking with Nelly by the park wall, slips over to retrieve a fallen hat and is accosted by Heathcliff. He accuses her of breaking Linton's heart, insisting his son is dying. Catherine determines to pay a secret visit.

Catherine and Nelly's visit takes place in **chapter twenty-three**. Sickly and self-absorbed, Linton tortures Catherine by exaggerating a violent coughing fit and forces her to stay and pamper him. Riding home Nelly catches a bad cold. She later discovers that during her three weeks in bed Catherine had vis-ited the Heights almost every evening. She extracts a confes-sion from Catherine after catching her returning from another visit. Catherine tells of Linton's temper and Hareton's bashful attentions and jealousy. Heathcliff appears to have been a hidden but watchful audience.

Nelly reports Catherine's visits to her father, who again puts an end to them. The months pass and Catherine turns seventeen. Her father, his health failing, worries for her future and agrees to let the cousins meet on the moors. At the first meeting Linton is so weak he can barely walk; he dozes off but wakes terrified that Nelly and Catherine should leave before the allotted time.

Catherine is saddened by the meeting, and the next week, in **chapter twenty-seven**, her father is so much worse that she sets out for her visit unwillingly. She meets Linton almost crazed with fear. Heathcliff appears, Linton falls limp, and Catherine is forced to help escort him to his house, while Nelly follows scolding. At the Heights Heathcliff, in his strongest incarnation of a Gothic villain, kidnaps Catherine. He locks the door and slaps her for resisting. Linton selfishly refuses to help her. Heathcliff forces Nelly and Catherine to stay overnight and in the morning takes Catherine away. Nelly remains locked up for five days. When she is set free she learns that Heathcliff has forced Catherine to marry Linton. Nelly leaves to get help and finds Edgar on his deathbed. That evening Catherine escapes and is able to sit by her father as he dies.

After the funeral Heathcliff arrives to take Catherine back to the Heights to nurse Linton, forbidding Nelly to see her. He also tells a horrified Nelly that, after Edgar's burial, he had dug up and opened Cathy's coffin. He tells how he has been haunted by her presence since the night of her funeral, when he had gone to the graveyard to dig up her coffin and had heard a distinct sigh at his ear. From that moment he had felt her presence constantly. "And when I slept in her chamber . . ." he recalls, "I couldn't lie there; for the moment I closed my eyes, she was either outside the window, or sliding back the panels, or entering the room. . . ." The sight of her still unmarred beauty has eased his tortured nerves.

Nelly learns only through hearsay of her mistress's new life. Catherine is forced to nurse Linton alone and lives a sleepless, grim existence until he dies. The experience turns her bitter and hostile. She rarely leaves her room unless driven out by cold. In the kitchen she antagonizes the housekeeper and reviles Hareton's acts of kindness. This dreary state of affairs brings the story up to the present: Lockwood has witnessed such scenes himself during his visits.

Here (**chapter thirty-one**) the frame narrative intervenes again. Lockwood's journal now dates from the second week of January 1802; he has recovered from his cold and is determined to leave his isolation for London. He pays a last visit to the Heights, meeting a low-spirited Catherine, who mourns for her old life and her books and cruelly taunts Hareton for his attempts to read. Heathcliff's entrance cuts an admiring Lockwood's overtures to Catherine short, and he soon leaves. The diary then leaps eight months to September of that year. Visiting in the neighborhood Lockwood finds himself near Thrushcross Grange and decides to spend the night. He finds Nelly has moved to the Heights, and on going to see her he learns that Heathcliff is dead and Catherine is engaged to marry Hareton. He first comes upon the lovers engrossed in a reading lesson. Hareton, happy and well groomed, dotes on his beautiful, playful teacher. Regretting his own lost chance, Lockwood sneaks off to find Nelly and hear the end of the story.

Nelly had been summoned to the Heights soon after Lockwood's departure. Her mistress, first delighted to see her, had soon grown irritable and impatient. She constantly sought out Hareton's company in order to tease him. She had tried underhandedly to entice him to read but he had stubbornly ignored her. Finally she had apologized to him, sealing her peace offering with a kiss and a book, gifts he could barely accept in his bashful confusion.

At the time this new alliance is formed, Heathcliff has begun to act strange and distant, increasingly attracted by a mysterious otherworldly force. He forgets to eat or sleep. One morning, after spending the night wandering the heath, he tells Nelly, "Last night I was on the threshold of hell. Today I am within sight of my heaven" (**chapter thirty-three**).

That morning he is startled by the sight of the happy couple, Catherine and Hareton, who share a marked likeness to the late Cathy—Hareton in particular resembles his aunt. Heathcliff confides to Nelly that Hareton reminds him uncannily of his former self. Here he makes explicit an important theme of the novel: the repeated pattern of the love affairs. Heathcliff admits to Nelly that the attachment is a "poor conclusion" to his plans, but that his altered state has sapped his desire for revenge. "I don't care for striking, I can't take the trouble to raise my hand."

Heathcliff's torturous, distracted existence continues. That evening Nelly takes fright on finding him transfixed in a deep reverie with ghastly sunken eyes and a menacing smile. His nocturnal wanderings continue and during the day he locks himself in Cathy's paneled bedroom. After a further night of wild storms Nelly breaks into the room to find the windows open, and when she pulls back the panels she is met with a fierce unblinking gaze—Heathcliff is dead. To the scandal of the community Heathcliff is buried next to Catherine. The country folk doubt that he rests in peace, claiming that they have seen his ghost walking the moors. Nelly is skeptical, although she herself has recently met a young shepherd boy on the heath who, sobbing, reported that he had just seen Heathcliff walking with a woman. The book ends with this final suggestion that Cathy and Heathcliff have been reunited in their moorland paradise.

In her novel Brontë thus allows the love affair of the second generation to be played out as a muted and happy version of the first. Nonetheless, it is Cathy and Heathcliff's love story which remains branded on the reader's memory. Their fiery example idealizes love as an attraction of equal, explosive forces, as a passion too savagely strong for the confines of cultivated society, and ultimately as a bond more powerful than life itself. ❖

—*Anna Guillemin*
Princeton University

List of Characters

Catherine (Cathy) Earnshaw is the beautiful, passionate, and destructive heroine of *Wuthering Heights*. She finds her soul mate in the dark, brooding Heathcliff but marries a much weaker man and destroys their happiness. She has grown up with Heathcliff, an adopted gypsy child, and their friendship strengthens during an orphaned adolescence under the tyrannical rule of her older brother. Defiant, domineering, and impetuous, Cathy finds a new admirer in the delicate, pampered Edgar Linton, but she grows delirious with grief when a spurned Heathcliff leaves the Heights. Her joy at his return, a year into her marriage to Edgar, is so great that her husband's jealousy is aroused. Violent arguments ensue, and Cathy self-destructively hastens her own end through rage and starvation. She dies in childbirth. Her spirit literally and figuratively haunts the rest of the novel. Heathcliff is tortured by her memory, farmers claim to see her ghost walking the moors, and the narrator himself encounters her frightening dream-figure. Cathy's tragedy also threatens until the last to haunt and repeat itself in the life of her daughter.

Heathcliff is the passionate, vengeful hero of Brontë's novel. His mysterious origin makes him a social outcast among the landed gentry, and his destitute adolescence creates a stoical, calculating temperament. He is Cathy's physical and spiritual equal, but when she accepts Edgar's attentions he deserts the Heights. He returns mysteriously rich and educated, destroying the equilibrium of Cathy's marriage. He elopes with Isabella Linton to destroy her brother, Edgar, and lures Hindley Earnshaw into gambling away his rights to Wuthering Heights. Heathcliff's thirst for revenge is only checked when he senses the imminence of his own death, and with it a final reunion with his ghostly beloved.

Nelly Dean is the housekeeper whose account of the events at Wuthering Heights comprise the body of the narrator's—Mr. Lockwood's—records. She is a sturdy local woman whose commonsensical nature contrasts sharply with the unfettered passions of her subjects. Having grown up in the Earnshaw household and served as Cathy's maid during her marriage,

Nelly has a privileged vantage point. She is a keen and critical observer who is not above listening at doors or reading letters. After Cathy's death, Nelly becomes the nursemaid of her daughter, Catherine, and witnesses the twists of fortunes of her new charge. She also witnesses Heathcliff's strange and ghostly death, which contradicts her own rational worldview.

Mr. Lockwood is the secondhand narrator of *Wuthering Heights:* the novel consists of his diary entries during a period as Heathcliff's tenant and records the story he hears from Nelly. Lockwood is a young London gentleman who rents the old Linton estate from Heathcliff and soon grows curious about his misanthropic landlord with the beautiful widowed daughter-in-law. Lockwood is little more than a passive listener, confined to his bed with a cold for most of the novel, yet his impartial facade unsuccessfully hides his admiration for the second Catherine Linton.

Edgar Linton is Cathy's husband. He is a soft, effeminate character, completely in the power of his willful, temperamental wife. He suffers through her rages and illnesses, and when she dies he resigns himself to an isolated life devoted to his daughter. His gentle, timorous nature contrasts entirely with vengeful Heathcliff's passion. His rival destroys his happiness a second time by kidnapping his adolescent daughter, Catherine. The blow is so devastating that Edgar soon dies of grief.

Isabella Linton is Edgar's younger sister. She is a pampered child and a selfish, reckless young woman. When Heathcliff returns, Isabella falls in love with him and they elope, despite her brother's prohibitions and Cathy's serious illness. She is shocked by Heathcliff's cruelty but counters with her own viciousness and flees the Heights on the night of Cathy's funeral, when Heathcliff is overcome by grief. Here she exits the story, moving to the south, giving birth to a son, and then dying twelve years later.

Hindley Earnshaw is Cathy's older brother and Heathcliff's hated enemy. He is jealous of Heathcliff as a child and tries to ruin him once he becomes master of Wuthering Heights. He reduces Heathcliff to abject poverty but falls into bad ways himself after his wife dies. When Heathcliff returns a rich gentleman after several years' absence, Hindley takes him in as a boarder to satiate his greed for gambling. He soon loses his entire estate at cards. Until his death Hindley leads a violent drunken existence indebted to his enemy.

Catherine Linton is Cathy's daughter and the heroine of the second half of the novel. She has both Edgar's gentleness, playing the devoted daughter during an idyllic childhood, and Cathy's willful haughtiness, which manifests itself during her enforced residence at the Heights. Heathcliff kidnaps her and forces her when she is sixteen to marry his dying son Linton. She is soon widowed, orphaned, and stripped of her inheritance, and her miserable life at the Heights begins to parallel that of her mother's under a tyrannical brother. The love she eventually discovers for her rough, illiterate cousin Hareton nonetheless leads to a brighter future.

Hareton Earnshaw is the son of Hindley, Cathy's older brother. When his mother dies soon after his birth, his father becomes a violent drunkard. Hareton grows up angry and unloved. Clear parallels are drawn between the downtrodden Hareton and the sullen young Heathcliff. Hareton's fate threatens to end tragically when the beautiful Catherine Linton arrives at the Heights and scorns her cousin's gestures of friendship. She eventually overcomes her prejudices and Heathcliff dies before he can destroy a union which returns Wuthering Heights to its rightful heir and matches the second generation's true hero and heroine.

Linton Heathcliff is Heathcliff's sickly son, the product of the unhappy union of Heathcliff and Isabella Linton. Raised for his first twelve years by his mother, he is taken to the Heights after her death. Linton is small-minded and cruel despite his physical weaknesses. Terrified of his father and acting only out of self-preservation, he helps Heathcliff to kidnap Catherine and marries her against her will. Linton soon dies, having impressed the reader with his petty selfishness, which stands in sharp contrast to Hareton's rough but well-meaning generosity. ❖

Critical Views

[Edwin P. Whipple (1819–1886) was one of the leading American literary critics and reviewers of the nine-teenth century. Among his many books are *Essays and Reviews* (1848) and *The Literature of the Age of Elizabeth* (1869). In this review of *Wuthering Heights,* Whipple speaks for many contemporary readers who felt that the novel's wild and passionate characters (especially Heathcliff) typified the "depravity" of the author, whom Whipple assumes to be a man.]

The truth is, that the whole firm of Bell & Co. seem to have a sense of the depravity of human nature peculiarly their own. It is the yahoo, not the demon, that they select for representa-tion; their Pandemonium is of mud rather than fire.

This is especially the case with Acton Bell, the author of *Wuthering Heights, The Tenant of Wildfell Hall,* and, if we mis-take not, of certain offensive but powerful portions of *Jane Eyre.* Acton, when left altogether to his own imaginations, seems to take a morose satisfaction in developing a full and complete science of human brutality. In *Wuthering Heights* he has succeeded in reaching the summit of this laudable ambition. He appears to think that spiritual wickedness is a combination of animal ferocities, and has accordingly made a compendium of the most striking qualities of tiger, wolf, cur, and wild-cat, in the hope of framing out of such elements a suitable brute-demon to serve as the hero of his novel. Compared with Heathcote, Squeers is considerate and Quilp humane. He is a deformed monster, whom the Mephistopheles of Goethe would have nothing to say to, whom the Satan of Milton would consider as an object of simple disgust, and to whom Dante would hesitate in awarding the honor of a place among those whom he has consigned to the burning pitch. This epitome of brutality, disavowed by man and devil, Mr. Acton Bell attempts in two whole volumes to delineate, and certainly he is to be congratulated on his success. As he is a man of uncommon talents, it is needless to say that it is to his subject and his dogged manner of handling it that we are to refer the burst of dislike with which the novel was received. His mode of delineating a bad character is to narrate every offensive act and repeat every vile expression which are characteristic. Hence, in *Wuthering Heights,* he details all the ingenuities of animal malignity, and exhausts the whole rhetoric of stupid blasphemy, in order that there may be no mistake as to the kind of person he intends to hold up to the popular gaze. Like all spendthrifts of malice and profanity, however, he overdoes the business. Though he scatters oaths as plentifully as sentimental writers do interjections, the comparative parsimony of the great novelists in this respect is productive of infinitely more effect. It must be confessed that this coarseness, though the prominent, is not the only characteristic of the writer. His attempt at originality does not stop with the conception of Heathcote, but he aims further to exhibit the action of the sentiment of love on the nature of the being whom his morbid imagination has created. This is by far the ablest and most subtile portion of his labors, and indicates that strong hold upon the elements of character, and that decision of touch in the delineation of the most evanescent qualities of emotion, which distinguish the mind of the whole family. For all practical purposes, however, the power evinced in *Wuthering Heights* is power thrown away. Nightmares and dreams, through which devils dance and wolves howl, make bad novels.

> —Edwin P. Whipple, "Novels of the Season," *North American Review* (October 1848): 357–59

❖

SYDNEY DOBELL ON THE CENTRAL CHARACTERS OF *WUTHERING HEIGHTS*

[Sydney Dobell (1824–1874) was a British poet and occasional critic. Among his nonfiction works are *Of Parliamentary Reform* (1865) and *Thoughts on Art,*

Philosophy, and Religion (1876). In this extract from a review of *Wuthering Heights,* Dobell examines Brontë's talent for characterization and praises her prose style.]

Laying aside *Wildfell Hall,* we open *Wuthering Heights,* as at once the earlier in date and ruder in execution. We look upon it as the flight of an impatient fancy fluttering in the very exultation of young wings; sometimes beating against its solitary bars, but turning, rather to exhaust, in a circumscribed space, the energy and agility which it may not yet spend in the heavens—a youthful story, written for oneself in solitude, and thrown aside till other successes recall the eyes to it in hope. In this thought let the critic take up the book; lay it down in what thought he will, there are some things in it he can lay down no more.

That Catherine Earnshaw—at once so wonderfully fresh, so fearfully natural—new, 'as if brought from other spheres,' and familiar as the recollection of some woeful experience—what can surpass the strange compatibility of her simultaneous loves; the involuntary art with which her two natures are so made to co-exist, that in the very arms of her lover we dare not doubt her purity; the inevitable belief with which we watch the oscillations of the old and new elements in her mind, and the exquisite truth of the last victory of nature over education, when the past returns to her as a flood, sweeping every modern landmark from within her, and the soul of the child, expanding, fills the woman?

Found at last, by her husband, insensible on the breast of her lover, and dying of the agony of their parting, one looks back upon her, like that husband, without one thought of accusation or absolution; her memory is chaste as the loyalty of love, pure as the air of the Heights on which she dwelt.

Heathcliff *might* have been as unique a creation. The conception in his case was as wonderfully strong and original, but he is spoilt in detail. The authoress has too often disgusted, where she should have terrified, and has allowed us a familiarity with her fiend which had ended in unequivocal contempt. If *Wuthering Heights* had been written as lately as *Jane Eyre,* the figure of Heathcliff, symmetrised and elevated, might have been one of the most natural and most striking portraits in the gallery of fiction.

Not a subordinate place or person in this novel but bears more or less the stamp of high genius. Ellen Dean is the ideal of the peasant playmate and servant of 'the family.' The substratum in which her mind moves is finely preserved. Joseph, as a specimen of the sixty years' servitor of 'the house,' is worthy a museum case. We feel that if Catherine Earnshaw bore her husband a child, it must be that Cathy Linton, and no other. The very Jane Eyre, of quiet satire, peeps out in such a paragraph as this:—'He told me to put on my cloak, and run to Gimmerton for the doctor and the parson. I went through wind and rain, and brought one, the doctor, back with me: the other said, *he would come in the morning.*' What terrible truth, what nicety of touch, what 'uncanny' capacity for mental aberration in the first symptoms of Catherine's delirium. 'I'm not wandering; you're mistaken, or else I should believe you really *were* that withered hag, and I should think I *was* under Penistone Crags: and I'm conscious it's night, and there are two candles on the table making the black press shine like jet.' What an unobtrusive, unexpected sense of *keeping* in the hanging of Isabella's dog.

The book abounds in such things. But one looks back at the whole story as to a world of brilliant figures in an atmosphere of mist; shapes that come out upon the eye, and burn their colours into the brain, and depart into the enveloping fog. It is the unformed writing of a giant's hand: the 'large utterance' of a baby god. In the sprawling of the infant Hercules, however, there must have been attitudes from which the statuary might model. In the early efforts of unusual genius, there are not seldom unconscious felicities which maturer years may look back upon with envy. The child's hand wanders over the strings. It cannot combine them in the chords and melodies of manhood; but its separate notes are perfect in themselves, and perhaps sound all the sweeter for the Æolian discords from which they come.

We repeat, that there are passages in this book of *Wuthering Heights* of which any novelist, past or present, might be proud.

Open the first volume at the fourteenth page, and read to the sixty-first. There are few things in modern prose to surpass these pages for native power. We cannot praise too warmly the brave simplicity, the unaffected air of intense belief, the admirable combination of extreme likelihood with the rarest originality, the nice provision of the possible even in the highest effects of the supernatural, the easy strength and instinct of keeping with which the accessory circumstances are grouped, the exquisite but unconscious art with which the chiaro-scuro of the whole is managed, and the ungenial frigidity of place, time, weather, and persons, is made to heighten the unspeakable pathos of one ungovernable outburst.

—Sydney Dobell, "Currer Bell" (1850), *The Life and Times of Sydney Dobell*, ed. Emily Jolly (1878), Vol. 1, pp. 169–71

❖

CHARLOTTE BRONTË ON SOME CRITICISMS OF *WUTHERING HEIGHTS*

[Charlotte Brontë (1816–1855) wrote the following preface to *Wuthering Heights* after her sister's death. Here, she examines some of the criticisms of the novel, arguing that some misunderstandings have arisen from readers' lack of familiarity with the author and the setting.]

With regard to the rusticity of *Wuthering Heights,* I admit the charge, for I feel the quality. It is rustic all through. It is moorish, and wild, and knotty as a root of heath. Nor was it natural that it should be otherwise; the author being herself a native and nursling of the moors. Doubtless, had her lot been cast in a town, her writings, if she had written at all, would have possessed another character. Even had chance or taste led her to choose a similar subject, she would have treated it otherwise. Had Ellis Bell been a lady or a gentleman accustomed to what is called "the world," her view of a remote and unreclaimed region, as well as of the dwellers therein, would have differed greatly from that actually taken by the home-bred country girl. Doubtless it would have been wider—more comprehensive: whether it would have been more original or more truthful is not so certain. As far as the scenery and locality are concerned, it could scarcely have been so sympathetic: Ellis Bell did not describe as one whose eye and taste alone found pleasure in the prospect; her native hills were far more to her than a spectacle; they were what she lived in, and by, as much as the wild birds, their tenants, or as the heather, their produce. Her descriptions, then, of natural scenery, are what they should be, and all they should be.

Where delineation of human character is concerned, the case is different. I am bound to avow that she had scarcely more practical knowledge of the peasantry amongst whom she lived, than a nun has of the country people who sometimes pass her convent gates. My sister's disposition was not naturally gregarious; circumstances favoured and fostered her tendency to seclusion; except to go to church or take a walk on the hills, she rarely crossed the threshold of home. Though her feeling for the people round was benevolent, intercourse with them she never sought; nor, with very few exceptions, ever experienced. And yet she knew them: knew their ways, their language, their family histories; she could hear of them with interest, and talk of them with detail, minute, graphic, and accurate; but *with* them, she rarely exchanged a word. Hence it ensued that what her mind had gathered of the real concerning them, was too exclusively confined to those tragic and terrible traits of which, in listening to the secret annals of every rude vicinage, the memory is sometimes compelled to receive the impress. Her imagination, which was a spirit more sombre than sunny, more powerful than sportive, found in such traits material whence it wrought creations like Heathcliff, like Earnshaw, like Catherine. Having formed these beings, she did not know what she had done. If the auditor of her work, when read in manuscript, shuddered under the grinding influence of natures so relentless and implacable, of spirits so lost and fallen; if it was complained that the mere hearing of certain vivid and fearful scenes banished sleep by night, and disturbed mental peace by day, Ellis Bell would wonder what was meant, and suspect the complainant of affectation. Had she but lived, her mind would of itself have grown like a strong tree, loftier, straighter, wider-spreading, and its matured fruits would have attained a mellower ripeness and sunnier bloom; but on that mind time and experience alone could work: to the influence of other intellects, it was not amenable.

Having avowed that over much of *Wuthering Heights* there broods "a horror of great darkness;" that is, in its storm-heated and electrical atmosphere, we seem at times to breathe lightning: let me point to those spots where clouded daylight and the eclipsed sun still attest their existence. For a specimen of true benevolence and homely fidelity, look at the character of Nelly Dean; for an example of constancy and tenderness, remark that of Edgar Linton. (Some people will think these qualities do not shine so well incarnate in a man as they would do in a woman, but Ellis Bell could never be brought to comprehend this notion: nothing moved her more than any insinuation that the faithfulness and clemency, the long-suffering and loving-kindness which are esteemed virtues in the daughters of Eve, become foibles in the sons of Adam. She held that mercy and forgiveness are the divinest attributes of the Great Being who made both man and woman, and that what clothes the Godhead in glory, can disgrace no form of feeble humanity). There is a dry saturnine humour in the delineation of old Joseph, and some glimpses of grace and gaiety animate the younger Catherine. Nor is even the first heroine of the name destitute of a certain strange beauty in her fierceness, or of honesty in the midst of perverted passion and passionate perversity. ⟨. . .⟩

Wuthering Heights was hewn in a wild workshop, with simple tools, out of homely materials. The statuary found a granite block on a solitary moor; gazing thereon, he saw how from the crag might be elicited a head, savage, swart, sinister; a form moulded with at least one element of grandeur—power. He wrought with a rude chisel, and from no model but the vision of his meditations. With time and labour, the crag took human shape; and there it stands colossal, dark, and frowning, half statue, half rock: in the former sense, terrible and goblin-like; in the latter, almost beautiful, for its colouring is of mellow grey, and moorland moss clothes it; and heath, with its blooming bells and balmy fragrance, grows faithfully close to the giant's foot.

—Charlotte Brontë, "Preface," *Wuthering Heights* [by Emily Brontë] *and Agnes Grey* [by Anne Brontë] (London: Smith, Elder & Co., 1850)

❖

ALGERNON CHARLES SWINBURNE ON THE PURITY OF PASSION IN *WUTHERING HEIGHTS*

[Algernon Charles Swinburne (1837–1909), a leading British poet and dramatist of the later nineteenth century, was also an important critic. He helped to create a revival of interest in Elizabethan and Jacobean drama with his studies of Christopher Marlowe (1883), Thomas Middleton (1887), and Cyril Tourneur (1889). In this extract, Swinburne connects the purity of passion in *Wuthering Heights* with Brontë's conception of the nobility of humanity.]

A graver and perhaps a somewhat more plausible charge is brought against the author of *Wuthering Heights* by those who find here and there in her book the savage note or the sickly symptom of a morbid ferocity. Twice or thrice especially the details of deliberate or passionate brutality in Heathcliff's treatment of his victims make the reader feel for a moment as though he were reading a police report or even a novel by some French 'naturalist' of the latest and brutallest order. But the pervading atmosphere of the book is so high and healthy that the effect even of those 'vivid and fearful scenes' which impaired the rest of Charlotte Brontë is almost at once neutralized—we may hardly say softened, but sweetened, dispersed, and transfigured—by the general impression of noble purity and passionate straightforwardness, which removes it at once and for ever from any such ugly possibility of association or comparison. The whole work is not more incomparable in the effect of its atmosphere or landscape than in the peculiar note of its wild and bitter pathos; but most of all is it unique in the special and distinctive character of its passion. The love which devours life itself, which devastates the present and desolates the future with unquenchable and raging fire, has nothing less pure in it than flame or sunlight. And this passionate and ardent chastity is utterly and unmistakably spontaneous and unconscious. Not till the story is ended, not till the effect of it has been thoroughly absorbed and digested, does the reader even perceive the simple and natural absence of any grosser element, any hint or suggestion of a baser alloy in the ingredients of its human emotion than in the splendour of lightning or the roll of a gathered wave. Then, as on issuing sometimes from the tumult of charging waters, he finds with something of wonder how absolutely pure and sweet was the element of living storm with which his own nature has been for awhile made one; not a grain in it of soiling sand, not a waif of clogging weed. As was the author's life, so is her book in all things; troubled and taintless, with little of rest in it, and nothing of reproach. It may be true that not many will ever take it to their hearts; it is certain that those who do like it will like nothing very much better in the whole world of poetry or prose.

—Algernon Charles Swinburne, "Emily Brontë" (1883), *Miscellanies* (London: Chatto & Windus, 1886), pp. 269–70

❖

MRS. HUMPHRY WARD ON ROMANTIC ELEMENTS IN *WUTHERING HEIGHTS*

[Mary A. Ward (1851–1920), better known as Mrs. Humphry Ward, was a widely published English novelist, biographer, critic, and political activist. In this extract, Ward discusses *Wuthering Heights* in the context of the Romantic movement of the period.]

Wuthering Heights is a book of the later Romantic movement, betraying the influences of German Romantic imagination, as Charlotte's work betrays the influences of Victor Hugo and

George Sand. The Romantic tendency to invent and delight in monsters, the *exaltation du moi,* which has been said to be the secret of the whole Romantic revolt against classical models and restraints; the love of violence in speech and action, the preference for the hideous in character and the abnormal in situation—of all these there are abundant examples in *Wuthering Heights.* The dream of Mr. Lockwood in Catherine's box bed, when in the terror of nightmare he pulled the wrist of the little wailing ghost outside on to the broken glass of the window, 'and rubbed it to and fro till the blood ran down and soaked the bed-clothes'—one of the most gruesome fancies of literature!—Heathcliff's long and fiendish revenge on Hindley Earnshaw; the ghastly quarrel between Linton and Heathcliff in Catherine's presence after Heathcliff's return; Catherine's three days' fast, and her delirium when she 'tore the pillow with her teeth;' Heathcliff dashing his head against the trees of her garden, leaving his blood upon the bark, and 'howling, not like a man, but like a savage beast being goaded to death with knives and spears;' the fight between Heathcliff and Earnshaw after Heathcliff's marriage to Isabella; the kidnapping of the younger Catherine, and the horror rather suggested than described of Heathcliff's brutality towards his sickly son:—all these things would not have been written precisely as they were written, but for the 'Germanism' of the thirties and forties, but for the translations of *Blackwood* and *Fraser,* and but for those German tales, whether of Hoffmann or others, which there is evidence that Emily Brontë read both at Brussels and after her return.

As to the 'exaltation of the Self,' its claims, sensibilities and passions, in defiance of all social law and duty, there is no more vivid expression of it throughout Romantic literature than is contained in the conversation between the elder Catherine and Nelly Dean before Catherine marries Edgar Linton. And the violent, clashing egotisms of Heathcliff and Catherine in the last scene of passion before Catherine's death, are as it were an epitome of a whole *genre* in literature, and a whole phase of European feeling.

Nevertheless, horror and extravagance are not really the characteristic mark and quality of *Wuthering Heights.* If they were, it would have no more claim upon us than a hundred other forgotten books—Lady Caroline Lamb's *Glenarvon* amongst them—which represent the dregs and refuse of a great literary movement. As in the case of Charlotte Brontë, the peculiar force of Emily's work lies in the fact that it represents the grafting of a European tradition upon a mind already richly stored with English and local reality, possessing at command a style at once strong and simple, capable both of homeliness and magnificence. The form of Romantic imagination which influenced Emily was not the same as that which influenced Charlotte; whether from a secret stubbornness and desire of difference, or no, there is not a mention of the French language, or of French books, in Emily's work, while Charlotte's abounds in a kind of display of French affinities, and French scholarship. The dithyrambs of *Shirley* and *Villette,* the 'Vision of Eve' of *Shirley,* and the desciption of Rachel in *Villette,* would have been impossible to Emily; they come to a great extent from the reading of Victor Hugo and George Sand. But in both sisters there is a similar *fonds* of stern and simple realism; a similar faculty of observation at once shrewd, and passionate; and it is by these that they produce their ultimate literary effect. The difference between them is almost wholly in Emily's favour. The uneven, amateurish manner of so many pages in *Jane Eyre* and *Shirley;* the lack of literary reticence which is responsible for Charlotte's frequent intrusion of her own personality, and for her occasional temptations to scream and preach, which are not wholly resisted even in her masterpiece *Villette;* the ugly tawdry sentences which disfigure some of her noblest passages, and make quotation from her so difficult:—you will find none of these things in *Wuthering Heights.* Emily is never flurried, never self-conscious; she is master of herself at the most rushing moments of feeling or narrative; her style is simple, sensuous, adequate and varied from first to last; she has fewer purple patches than Charlotte, but at its best, her insight no less than her power of phrase, is of a diviner and more exquisite quality.

—Mrs. Humphry Ward, "Introduction," *Wuthering Heights*
(New York: Harper & Brothers, 1900), pp. xxv–xxvii

♣

W. D. HOWELLS ON HEROINES IN CHARLOTTE AND EMILY BRONTË'S WORKS

[W. D. Howells (1837–1920), a leading American novelist, was also a prolific critic and frequent contributor of articles and reviews to the *Atlantic Monthly* and *Harper's Magazine*. His critical works include *Criticism and Fiction* (1891), *My Literary Passions* (1895), and *Literature and Life* (1902). In this extract, Howells compares the heroines of Emily and Charlotte Brontë, finding great power in the latter's creations in spite of their seeming defiance of conventional realistic standards.]

The heroines of Emily Brontë have not the artistic completeness of Charlotte Brontë's. They are blocked out with hysterical force, and in their character there is something elemental, as if, like the man who beat and browbeat them, they too were close to the savagery of nature. The sort of supernaturalism, which appears here and there in their story, wants the refinement of the telepathy and presentiment which play a part in Jane Eyre, but it is still more effectual in the ruder clutch which it lays upon the fancy.

In her dealing with the wild passion of Heathcliff for the first Catharine, Emily Brontë does not keep even such slight terms with convention as Charlotte does in the love of Rochester and Jane Eyre; but this fierce longing, stated as it were in its own language, is still farther from anything that corrupts or tempts; it is as wholesome and decent as a thunder-storm, in the consciousness of the witness. The perversities of the mutual attraction of the lovers are rendered without apparent sense on the part of the author that they can seem out of nature, so deeply does she feel them to be in nature, and there is no hint from her that they need any sort of proof. It is vouchsafed us to know that Heathcliff is a foundling of unknown origin, early fixed in his hereditary evils by the cruelty of Hindley Earnshaw, whose father has adopted him; but it is not explained why he should have his malign power upon Catharine. Perhaps it is enough that she is shown a wilful, impetuous, undisciplined girl, whose pity has been moved for the outcast before her fancy is taken. After that we are told what happens and are left to account for it as we may.

We are very badly told, in terms of autobiography thrice involved. First, we have the narrative of Heathcliff's tenant, then within his the narrative of the tenant's housekeeper, as she explains the situation she has witnessed at Heathcliff's house, and then within hers the several narratives of the actors in the tragedy. Seldom has a great romance been worse contrived, both as to generals and particulars, but the essentials are all there, and the book has a tremendous vitality. If it were of the fashion of any other book, it might have passed away, but it is of its own fashion solely, and it endures like a piece of the country in which its scenes are laid, enveloped in a lurid light and tempestuous atmosphere of its own. Its people are all of extreme types, and yet they do not seem unreal, like the extravagant creations of Dickens's fancy; they have an intense and convincing reality, the weak ones, such as Heathcliff's wife and son, equally with the powerful, such as Heathcliff himself and the Catharines, mother and daughter. A weird malevolence broods over the gloomy drama, and through all plays a force truly demoniacal, with scarcely the relief of a moment's kindliness. The facts are simply conceived, and stated without shadow of apology or extenuation; and the imagination from which they sprang cannot adequately be called morbid, for it deals with the brute motives employed without a taint of sickly subjectiveness. The author remains throughout superior to her material; her creations have all a distinct projection, and in this, Emily Brontë shows herself a greater talent than Charlotte, who is never quite detached from her heroine, but is always trammelled in sympathy with Jane Eyre, with whom she is united by ties of a like vocation and experience, as governess. You feel that she is present in all Jane's sufferings, small and great, if not in her raptures; but Emily Brontë keeps as sternly aloof from both her Catharines as from Heathcliff himself. She bequeathed the world at her early death a single book of as singular power as any in fiction; and proved herself, in spite of its defective technique, a great artist, of as realistic motive and ideal as any who have followed her.

—W. D. Howells, "Heroines of Nineteenth-Century Fiction: XIX. The Two Catherines of Emily Brontë," *Harper's Bazaar,* 29 December 1900, pp. 2224–25

♣

[May Sinclair (1863–1946), a British novelist, biographer, and critic, wrote such works as *A Defence of Idealism* (1917) and *The Three Brontës* (1912), from which the following extract is taken. Here, Sinclair explores the nature of Heathcliff's vengeance, arguing that it is a thing altogether inhuman.]

Hindley Earnshaw is brutal to the foundling, Heathcliff, and degrades him. Heathcliff, when his hour comes, pays back his wrong with the interest due. He is brutal beyond brutality to Hindley Earnshaw, and he degrades Hareton, Hindley's son, as he himself was degraded; but he is not brutal to him. The frustrated passion of Catherine Earnshaw for Heathcliff, and of Heathcliff for Catherine, hardly knows itself from hate; they pay each other back torture for torture, and pang for hopeless pang. When Catherine marries Edgar Linton, Heathcliff marries Isabella, Edgar's sister, in order that he may torture to perfection Catherine and Edgar and Isabella. His justice is more than poetic. The love of Catherine Earnshaw was all that he possessed. He knows that he has lost it through the degradation that he owes to Hindley Earnshaw. It is because an Earnshaw and a Linton between them have robbed him of all that he possessed, that, when his hour comes, he pays himself back by robbing the Lintons and the Earnshaws of all that *they* possess, their Thrushcross Grange and Wuthering Heights. He loathes above all loathly creatures, Linton, his own son by Isabella. The white-blooded thing is so sickly that he can hardly keep it alive. But with an unearthly cruelty he cherishes, he nourishes this spawn till he can marry it on its death-bed to the younger Catherine, the child of Catherine Earnshaw and of Edgar Linton. This supreme deed accomplished, he lets the creature die, so that Thrushcross Grange may fall into his hands. Judged by his bare deeds, Heathcliff seems a monster of evil, a devil without any fiery infernal splendour, a mean and sordid devil.

But—and this is what makes Emily Brontë's work stupendous—not for a moment can you judge Heathcliff by his bare deeds. Properly speaking, there are no bare deeds to judge him by. Each deed comes wrapt in its own infernal glamour, trailing a cloud of supernatural splendor. The whole drama moves on a plane of reality superior to any deed. The spirit of it, like Emily Brontë's spirit, is superbly regardless of the material event. As far as material action goes Heathcliff is singularly inert. He never seems to raise a hand to help his vengeance. He lets things take their course. He lets Catherine marry Edgar Linton and remain married to him. He lets Isabella's passion satisfy itself. He lets Hindley Earnshaw drink himself to death. He lets Hareton sink to the level of a boor. He lets Linton die. His most overt and violent action is the capture of the younger Catherine. And even there he takes advantage of the accident that brings her to the door of Wuthering Heights. He watches and bides his time with the intentness of a brooding spirit that in all material happenings seeks its own. He makes them his instruments of vengeance. And Heathcliff's vengeance, like his passion for Catherine, is an immortal and immaterial thing. He shows how little he thinks of sordid, tangible possession; for, when his vengeance is complete, when Edgar Linton and Linton Heathcliff are dead and their lands and houses are his, he becomes utterly indifferent. He falls into a melancholy. He neither eats nor drinks. He shuts himself up in Cathy's little room and is found dead there, lying on Cathy's bed.

—May Sinclair, *The Three Brontës* (London: Hutchinson, 1912), pp. 244–46

❖

E. M. FORSTER ON EMOTIONAL CHAOS IN *WUTHERING HEIGHTS*

[E. M. Forster (1879–1970), one of the most influential British novelists of the twentieth century, was also an important critic. Among his works of criticism are *Abinger Harvest* (1924), *Two Cheers for Democracy* (1951), and *Aspects of the Novel* (1927), from which the following extract is taken. Here, Forster argues that it is the emotional chaos exhibited by Catherine and Heathcliff that gives *Wuthering Heights* its power.]

⟨. . .⟩ the emotions of Heathcliffe and Catherine Earnshaw function differently to other emotions in fiction. Instead of inhabiting the characters, they surround them like thunder clouds, and generate the explosions that fill the novel from the moment when Lockwood dreams of the hand at the window down to the moment when Heathcliffe, with the same window open, is discovered dead. *Wuthering Heights* is filled with sound— storm and rushing wind—a sound more important than words and thoughts. Great as the novel is, one cannot afterwards remember anything in it but Heathcliffe and the elder Catherine. They cause the action by their separation: they close it by their union after death. No wonder they "walk"; what else could such beings do? even when they were alive their love and hate transcended them.

Emily Brontë had in some ways a literal and careful mind. She constructed her novel on a time chart even more elaborate than Miss Austen's, and she arranged the Linton and Earnshaw families symmetrically, and she had a clear idea of the various legal steps by which Heathcliffe gained possession of their two properties. Then why did she deliberately introduce muddle, chaos, tempest? Because in our sense of the word she was a prophetess: because what is implied is more important to her than what is said; and only in confusion could the figures of Heathcliffe and Catherine externalize their passion till it streamed through the house and over the moors. *Wuthering Heights* has no mythology beyond what these two characters provide: no great book is more cut off from the universals of Heaven and Hell. It is local, like the spirits it engenders, and whereas we may meet Moby Dick in any pond, we shall only encounter them among the harebells and limestone of their own county.

—E. M. Forster, "Prophecy," *Aspects of the Novel* (New York: Harcourt, Brace & World, 1927), pp. 209–11

❖

V. S. PRITCHETT ON UNITY WITH NATURE IN *WUTHERING HEIGHTS*

[V. S. Pritchett (b. 1900), a British novelist and short story writer, is also an important literary critic. He is the author of *The Living Novel* (1946) and of critical studies of Balzac (1973) and Turgenev (1977). In this extract, Pritchett argues that the power of *Wuthering Heights* rests in the fact that Brontë rejects civilized society altogether and portrays humanity in unity with nature.]

There is no other novel in the English language like *Wuthering Heights.* It is unique first of all for its lack of psychological dismay. Never, in a novel, did so many people hate each other with such zest, such Northern zest. There is a faint, homely pretence that Nelly, the housekeeper and narrator, is a kindly, garrulous old body; but look at her. It is not concealed that she is a spy, a go-between, a secret opener of letters. She is a wonderful character, as clear and round as any old nurse in Richardson or Scott; but no conventional sentiment encases her. She is as hard as iron and takes up her station automatically in the battle. Everyone hates, no one disguises evil in this book; no one is "nice." How refreshing it is to come across a Victorian novel which does not moralise, and yet is very far from amoral. How strange, in Victorian fiction, to see passion treated as the natural pattern of life. How refreshing to see the open skirmishing of egotism, and to see life crackling like a fire through human beings; a book which *feels* human beings as they feel to themselves.

And that brings us to the more important difference between *Wuthering Heights* and the other English novels of the nineteenth century: Emily Brontë is not concerned with man and society, but with his unity with nature. He, too, is a natural force, not the product of a class. Her view is altogether primitive. Often wild romanticism, the fiery murk of the Gothic revival, threaten to impair her picture; but these literary echoes are momentary. Her spirit is naturally pagan and she appears to owe nothing at all to the general traditions of our novel which has fed upon the sociability of men and women and the preaching of reform. (D. H. Lawrence, who used to be compared with her in the heyday of mysticism twenty years back, is utterly cut off from her by his preaching, by the nonconformist ache.) This isolation of Emily Brontë is startling, and only Conrad and Henry James, in their very different ways, were parallel to her. Here perhaps lies a clue: they were foreigners who were crossed with us. By some Mendelian accident, Emily

Brontë seems to have reverted to the Irish strain in the Brontë family and to have slipped back, in the isolation and intense life of the Yorkshire moors, to an earlier civilisation. She is pre-Christian. The vision of the union of man and nature is natural to her. Or rather, as in many writers of split racial personality, one sees two countries, two civilisations, two social histories in conflict.

—V. S. Pritchett, "Books in General," *New Statesman and Nation,* 22 June 1946, p. 453

❖

DOROTHY VAN GHENT ON HEATHCLIFF AS ARCHETYPAL DEMON

[Dorothy Van Ghent (b. 1907) is the author of *Willa Cather* (1964) and *Keats: The Myth of the Hero* (1983). In this extract, Van Ghent explores the "otherness" or supernatural characteristics of Heathcliff, arguing that he fits into a traditional archetype of the outsider.]

There is still the difficulty of defining, with any precision, the quality of the daemonic that is realized most vividly in the conception of Heathcliff, a difficulty that is mainly due to our tendency always to give the "daemonic" some ethical status—that is, to relate it to an ethical hierarchy. Heathcliff's is an archetypal figure, untraceably ancient in mythological thought—an imaged recognition of that part of nature which is "other" than the human soul (the world of the elements and the animals) and of that part of the soul itself which is "other" than the conscious part. But since Martin Luther's revival of this archetype for modern mythology, it has tended to forget its relationship with the elemental "otherness" of the outer world and to identify itself solely with the dark functions of the soul. As an image of soul work, it is ethically relevant, since everything that the soul does—even unconsciously, even "ignorantly" (as in the case of Oedipus)—offers itself for ethical judgment, whereas the elements and the animals do not. Puritanism perpetuated the figure for the imagination; Milton gave it its greatest aesthetic splendor, in the fallen angel through whom the divine beauty still shone; Richardson introduced it, in the person of Lovelace, to an infatuated middle class; and always the figure was ethically relevant through the conception of "sin" and "guilt." (Let us note here, however, the ambivalence of the figure, an ambivalence that the medieval devil does not have. The medieval devil is a really ugly customer, so ugly that he can even become a comedy figure—as in the medieval moralities. The daemonic archetype of which we are speaking here is deeply serious in quality because of his ambivalence: he is a fertilizing energy and profoundly attractive, and at the same time horribly destructive to civilized institutionalism. It is because of his ambivalence that, though he is the "enemy," ethically speaking, he so easily takes on the stature and beauty of a hero, as he does in the Satan of *Paradise Lost.*) In Byron's *Manfred,* the archetype underwent a rather confusing sea-change, for Manfred's crime is, presumably, so frightful that it cannot be mentioned, and the indefinable nature of the crime blurs the edges of the figure and cuts down its resonance in the imagination (when we guess that the crime might be incest, we are disposed to find this a rather paltry equation for the Byronic incantation of guilt); nevertheless, the ethical relevancy of the figure remains. Let us follow it a little further, before returning to Emily Brontë's Heathcliff. In the later nineteenth century, in the novels of Dostoevski, it reappears with an enormous development of psychological subtlety, and also with a great strengthening and clarification of its ethical significance. In the work of André Gide, it undergoes another sea-change: the archetypal daemonic figure now becomes the principle of progress, the spirit of free investigation and creative experience; with this reorientation, it becomes positively ethical rather than negatively so. In Thomas Mann's. *Doctor Faustus,* it reverts to its earlier and more constant significance, as the type of the instinctive part of the soul, a great and fertilizing power, but ethically unregenerate and therefore a great danger to ethical man.

Our interest in sketching some phases of the history of this archetype has been to show that it has had, in modern mythology, constantly a status in relation to ethical thought. The exception is Heathcliff. Heathcliff is no more ethically relevant than is flood or earthquake or whirlwind. It is as impossible to speak of him in terms of "sin" and "guilt" as it is to speak in this way of the natural elements or the creatures of the animal world. In him, the type reverts to a more ancient mythology and to an earlier symbolism. *Wuthering Heights* so baffles and confounds the ethical sense because it is not informed with that sense at all: it is profoundly informed with the attitudes of "animism," by which the natural world—that world which is "other" than and "outside of" the consciously individualized human—*appears* to act with an energy similar to the energies of the soul; to be permeated with soul energy but of a mysterious and alien kind that the conscious human soul, bent on securing itself through civilization, cannot identify itself with as to purpose; an energy that can be propitiated, that can at times be canalized into humanly purposeful channels, that *must* be given religious recognition both for its enormous fertility and its enormous potential destructiveness. But Heathcliff does have human shape and human relationships; he is, so to speak, "caught in" the human; two kinds of reality intersect in him—as they do, with a somewhat different balance, in Catherine; as they do, indeed, in the other characters. Each entertains, in some degree, the powers of darkness—from Hindley, with his passion for self-destruction (he, too, wants to get "out"), to Nelly Dean, who in a sense "propitiates" those powers with the casuistry of her actions, and even to Lockwood, with his sadistic dream. Even in the weakest of these souls there is an intimation of the dark Otherness, by which the soul is related psychologically to the inhuman world of pure energy, for it carries within itself an "otherness" of its own, that inhabits below consciousness.

—Dorothy Van Ghent, "On *Wuthering Heights*," *The English Novel: Form and Function* (New York: Rinehart & Co., 1953), pp. 163–65

❖

J. Hillis Miller on Heathcliff's Sadism

[J. Hillis Miller (b. 1928) is chairman of the English department at Yale University and a leading literary critic and theorist. He is the author of *Fiction and Repetition* (1982), *The Linguistic Moment: From Wordsworth to Stevens* (1985), and *Theory Then and Now* (1991). In this extract, Miller investigates Heathcliff's sadistic relationship with Catherine, believing that his attempt to possess Catherine is an attempt to re-enter society.]

Heathcliff's situation after Cathy's death is different from hers while she lived, and his reaction to that situation is not the despairing acceptance of separateness, but the attempt to regain his lost fullness of being. The universal human desire is for union with something outside oneself. People differ from one another only in the intensity of their desire, and in the diversity of the ways they seek to assuage it.

After Cathy's death Heathcliff's whole life is concentrated on the suffering caused by his loss, and on the violence of his desire to get her back, for she is his soul, and without her he grovels in an abyss of nothingness. Why does Heathcliff spend so much of his time in an elaborate attempt to destroy Thrushcross Grange and Wuthering Heights, with all their inhabitants? Why does he take delight in torturing Hindley, Isabella, Hareton, the second Cathy, his son Linton? Why does he, both before Cathy's death and after, enter on a violent career of sadistic destruction? Is it because he is, as Cathy says, a "fierce, pitiless, wolfish man," or does his sadism have some further meaning?

During the violent scene of mutual recrimination between Heathcliff and Cathy which ends in the fight between Heathcliff and Edgar, Heathcliff tells Cathy that she has treated him "infernally" by betraying him and marrying Edgar. He will not, he says, "suffer unrevenged." But, says Heathcliff, "I seek no revenge on you . . . The tyrant grinds down his slaves and they don't turn against him, they crush those beneath them—You are welcome to torture me to death for your amusement, only, allow me to amuse myself a little in the same style . . ."

Heathcliff's cruelty toward others is a mode of relation to Cathy. Though his appearance at Wuthering Heights in itself disrupts the Earnshaw family, Heathcliff's relation to Cathy forms the basis of his defiance of everyone else, and his destructive hatred attains its full development only after he is separated from her. His sadistic treatment of others is the only kind of revenge against Cathy he can take, for the person who most controls events in *Wuthering Heights* is not Heathcliff. It is Cathy herself.

Heathcliff's sadism is more than an attempt to take revenge indirectly on Cathy. It is also a strange and paradoxical attempt to regain his lost intimacy with her. If Cathy can say, "I *am* Heathcliff," Heathcliff could equally well say, "I *am* Cathy," for she is, as he says, his "soul." Possession of Healthcliff gives Cathy possession of the entire universe. If she were to lose Heathcliff, "the universe would turn to a mighty stranger," just as Heathcliff becomes an alien and outcast from all the world after he loses Cathy. If his childhood relation to Cathy gave him possession of the whole world through her, perhaps now that Cathy is lost he can get her back by appropriating the world. The sadistic infliction of pain on other people, like the destruction of inanimate objects, is a way of breaking down the barriers between oneself and the world. Now that he has lost Cathy, the only thing remaining to Heathcliff which is like the lost fusion with her is the destructive assimilation of other people or things. So he turns sadist, just as, in the Gondal poems, Julius Brenzaida turns on the world in war when he has been betrayed by Augusta. Heathcliff's violence against everyone but Cathy plays the same role in *Wuthering Heights* as does the theme of war in the poems. In both cases there is an implicit recognition that war or sadism is like love because love too is destructive, since it must break down the separateness of the loved one. Augusta too is a sadist. She moves quickly from inspiring her lovers to abandon honor for her sake to betraying them and causing them to suffer. Like love, sadism is a moment of communion, a moment when the barriers between person and person are broken down. The climax of sadistic joy is loss of the sense of separateness. It is as though the person who is forced to suffer had lost his limits and had melted into the whole universe. At the same moment the self of the sadist dissolves too, and self and universe become one. Heathcliff's relation to Cathy has been fusion with the whole world through her. He feels that he can reverse the process and regain her by assimilating the world, for his sole aim is to "dissolve with" Cathy and be happy at last. Now he proposes to do this by getting control of Wuthering Heights and Thrushcross Grange in order to destroy them both. "I wish," says Heathcliff of his property, "I could annihilate it from the face of the earth." So he gives himself wholeheartedly to acts of sadistic destruction. No other figure in English literature takes so much pleasure in causing pain to others: "I have no pity! I have no pity!" he cries. "The more the worms writhe, the more I yearn to crush out their entrails! It is a moral teething, and I grind with greater energy, in proportion to the increase of pain." In another place he tells Nelly his feelings about his son and the second Cathy: "It's odd what a savage feeling I have to anything that seems afraid of me! Had I been born where laws are less strict, and tastes less dainty, I should treat myself to a slow vivisection of those two, as an evening's amusement."

Heathcliff's effort to regain Cathy through sadistic destruction fails, just as does Augusta's attempt to achieve through sadistic love a fusion with something outside herself, and just as does Cathy's decision to will her own death. Heathcliff's sadism fails because, as things or people are annihilated under the blows of the sadist, he is left with nothing. He reaches only an exacerbated sense of the absence of the longed-for intimacy rather than the intimacy itself. Augusta goes from lover to lover, destroying them one by one because she cannot reach what she wants through them. And Heathcliff finds that his career of sadistic revenge is a way of suffering the loss of Cathy more painfully rather than a way of reaching her again. "It is a poor conclusion, is it not," he asks. "An absurd termination to my violent exertions? I get levers, and mattocks to demolish the two houses, and train myself to be capable of working like Hercules, and when everything is ready, and in my power, I find the will to lift a slate off either roof has vanished! . . . I have lost the faculty of enjoying their destruction . . ."

The reason Heathcliff gives for having lost the will to demolish the two houses is a confirmation of the fact that his relation to everything in the world is a relation to Cathy, and an admission of the defeat of his attempt to regain her by destroying the Grange and the Heights. He says that everything in the universe is a reminder that Cathy has existed and that he does not possess her. Through his destruction of others he has reached, in the wreckage left after his violence, the full realization of her absence: ". . . what is not connnected with her to me?" he asks, "and what does not recall her? I cannot look down to this floor, but her features are shaped in the flags! In every cloud, in every tree—filling the air at night, and caught by glimpses in every object, by day I am surrounded with her image! The most ordinary faces of men, and women—my own features mock me with a resemblance. The entire world is a dreadful collection of memoranda that she did exist, and that I have lost her!" The universe is identified not with Cathy, but with the absence of Cathy, and to possess the world through its destructive appropriation is not to possess Cathy, but to confront once more the vacant place where she is not. This is the hell in which Heathcliff lives after her death: "I could *almost* see her, and yet I *could not!* I ought to have sweat blood then, from the anguish of my yearning, from the fervour of my supplications to have but one glimpse! I had not one. She showed herself, as she often was in life, a devil to me! And, since then, sometimes more, and sometimes less, I've been the sport of that intolerable torture!" Heathcliff's sadistic tormenting of others only leads him to be the more tormented, tormented by a Cathy whose strongest weapon is her invisibility.

—J. Hillis Miller, "Emily Brontë," *The Disappearance of God: Five Nineteenth-Century Writers* (Cambridge, MA: Harvard University Press, 1963), pp. 194–97

❧

DENIS DONOGHUE ON THRUSHCROSS GRANGE AND WUTHERING HEIGHTS

[Denis Donoghue (b. 1928) is an Irish-born literary critic and the author of many books, including *The Sovereign Ghost: Studies in Imagination* (1976), *We Irish: Essays on Irish Literature and Society* (1984), and *England, Their England: Commentaries on English Language and*

Literature (1988). He is Henry James Professor of Letters at New York University. In this extract, Donoghue compares the differing moral and social values represented by Thrushcross Grange and Wuthering Heights, the former residence standing for rational, civilized values, the latter for imagination and superstition.]

Catherine and Heathcliff are allowed to persevere in their natures; they are not forced to conform to the worldly proprieties of Thrushcross Grange. Conformity is reserved for the next generation. But this is too blunt as an account of the later chapters of the book. The juxtaposition of Wuthering Heights and Thrushcross Grange is inescapable, but it is not simple. The values of the Grange are social, political, personal, compatible with the emerging England, the cities, railways, the lapse of the old agricultural verities. Wuthering Heights is, in this relation, primitive, aboriginal, Bohemian; it rejects any pattern of action and relationships already prescribed. Finally, Emily Brontë accepts the dominance of Thrushcross Grange, since the new England requires that victory, but she accepts it with notable reluctance. Wuthering Heights has been presented as, in many respects, a monstrous place, but its violence is the mark of its own spirit, and Emily Brontë is slow to deny it. The entire book may be read as Emily Brontë's progress toward Thrushcross Grange, but only if the reading acknowledges the inordinate force of attraction, for her, in the Heights. We mark this allegiance when we associate the Heights with childhood, the Grange with adult compulsions. The Heights is also the place of soul, the Grange of body. Imagination, the will, the animal life, folk-wisdom, lore, superstition, ghosts: these are at home in the Heights. The Grange houses reason, formality, thinner blood. Much of this opposition is directed upon the question of education. Heathcliff is not a reader, Edgar is despised for his bookishness; but, at the end, the new generation resolves its quarrel in a shared book. I take this to mean that you must learn to read if you want to marry and live in the Grange. The young Cathy teaches Hareton to read, and thus redeems him. Emily Brontë endorses the change, but again with some reluctance, as if the Gutenberg civilization, inevitably successful, meant the death of other values dear to her. The end of the book is an image of concord, but we are meant to register the loss, too. This is implicit in the composition of the book. The fiction is Emily Brontë's composition, her assertion, and in a sense her act of defiance—set against the demonstrable success of fact, time, history, and the public world. At the end, Catherine and Hareton are to marry and, on New Year's Day, to move to the Grange. As for Wuthering Heights, another writer would have burnt it to the ground, but Emily Brontë retains it, in a measure. Joseph will take care of the house, meaning the living rooms, "and perhaps a lad to keep him company." As Mrs. Dean says, "they will live in the kitchen, and the rest will be shut up." The tone of this passage makes it clear that much of Emily Brontë's imagination remains at Wuthering Heights, not as a ghost to haunt it, but as a mind to respect it. It has been argued that we are not to choose between the two houses, but rather to hold them together in the mind. At the end, we choose, as Emily Brontë chose, as Cathy and Hareton chose; but we make the choice with reluctance and with a sense of the values which are inevitably lost. Wuthering Heights is not merely the terrible place of Lockwood's visits, not merely the result of rough manners, bad education, a gnarled landscape. Its chief characteristic is that it exists in its own right, by a natural law formulated, as it were, centuries before the laws of man and society. To that extent, it is closer than Thrushcross Grange to those motives and imperatives which, helplessly, we call Nature. That is its strength. We should not feel embarrassed by the violence of the first part of the book; it is neither melodramatic nor spurious. The energy dramatized there has nothing to sustain it but itself: hence its association with the elements, especially with wind, water, and fire, and with animals, dogs, snow. It is linked also to the landscape, the firs permanently slanted by the wind. "My love for Heathcliff," Catherine says, "resembles the eternal rocks beneath—a source of little visible delight, but necessary." The sentence provides a motto for the entire book, the acknowledgment of quality and character followed by appeal to an older law: necessity.

—Denis Donoghue, "Emily Brontë: On the Latitude of Interpretation," *The Interpretation of Narrative: Theory and Practice,* ed. Morton W. Bloomfield (Cambridge, MA: Harvard University Press, 1970), pp. 131–32

❖

[Arnold Krupat (b. 1941) is a professor of English and director of American studies at Sarah Lawrence College. He is the author of *For Those Who Come After: A Study of Native American Autobiography* (1985) and *Ethnocriticism: Ethnography, History, Literature* (1992). In this extract, Krupat argues that the development of Heathcliff's diction from gibberish to weariness is a tool Brontë used to convey the wildness of the world inhabited by the characters of *Wuthering Heights*.]

That Miss Brontë might have given us narrators with a more interesting or important style, that she could perfectly well have imagined speech more appropriate than any Nelly and Lockwood can produce is clear from the speech of almost all of the other characters, but foremost from the speech assigned to Heathcliff. Heathcliff's diction is precisely not fixed and unshakable, nor is it fully formed from the start. His style has a certain development throughout the novel.

Heathcliff's first words as a child are described as "gibberish that nobody could understand," and his last words are a curse of sorts. In between are many modulations. Almost always rough and violent, Heathcliff can nevertheless speak politely, even wittily; near the end of his life the roughness and violence begin to alternate with tones of weariness. Heathcliff's voice also has an element of unpredictability largely lacking in Nelly's and Lockwood's; we can guess the words that will accompany his responses to events rather less well than we can guess theirs.

Among the other characters, we may note briefly that Catherine Earnshaw's diction is not fixed either; yet she dies halfway through the book, before we can hear her speak to as many occasions as we would like. Hareton's diction also has a development, but in his case, similarly, we stop hearing the voice—for the book ends—just as its development seems likely to become interesting. These characters, too, tend more to occasional speechlessness than do either Nelly or Lockwood, as if to testify to the possibility that some responses to some experiences may be incapable of verbalization, that the world may not always be manageable—at least not in words. From them we hear speech often as strange as the experience it seeks to deal with.

The point, of course, is that Emily Brontë chose to give us little of Heathcliff's sort of speech and much of Nelly's and Lockwood's. One reason for this ⟨. . .⟩ is that to develop at length a highly distinctive diction consistent with highly distinctive materials is always to some extent to tame those materials. Simply to maintain such a special style (like Melville's or Faulkner's, for example) at length is to assert that strangeness can be contained, shaped, and ordered—or at least survived. But this is not what Emily Brontë wished to do, nor has it been the effect of her method. The effect of what she has done has been to leave the world wild, for it is just the wildness of the world, its untamable strangeness, that all of us have felt in *Wuthering Heights.* To have conveyed a vast, shapeless sense of things in a thing beautifully limited and shaped is the peculiar effect of Emily Brontë's technique. And the chief strategy of her technique is the persistent split between the materials of the book and the style in which they are presented.

—Arnold Krupat, "The Strangeness of *Wuthering Heights,*" *Nineteenth-Century Fiction* 25, No. 3 (December 1970): 279–80

❧

CAROLYN G. HEILBRUN ON ANDROGYNY IN *WUTHERING HEIGHTS*

[Carolyn G. Heilbrun (b. 1926) is the Avalon Foundation Professor of the Humanities at Columbia University. She is the author of *Christopher Isherwood* (1970), *Reinventing Womanhood* (1979), and *Hamlet's Mother and Other Women* (1990). Under her pseudonym Amanda Cross, she has written many mystery novels. In this extract, Heilbrun maintains that the relationship between Catherine and Heathcliff represents a perfect state of androgyny, which is later destroyed by Catherine's submission to her feminine side.]

The androgynous view of the novel is not meant to supplant but to accompany other interpretations of *Wuthering Heights.*

Indeed, the androgynous interpretation is simple enough. Catherine and Heathcliff, whose love represents the ultimate, apparently undefined, androgynous ideal, betray that love, or are betrayed by the world into deserting it. Nor is it insignificant that it is Catherine who at the same time articulates her oneness with Heathcliff and is tempted to betray the masculine half of her soul. Catherine refutes heaven, which is not her home: "I broke my heart with weeping to come back to earth," she tells Nelly, "and the angels were so angry that they flung me out, into the middle of the heath on the top of Wuthering Heights, where I woke sobbing for joy. That will do to explain my secret, as well as the other. I've no more business to marry Edgar Linton than I have to be in heaven; and if the wicked man in there had not brought Heathcliff so low, I shouldn't have thought of it. It would degrade me to marry Heathcliff now; so he shall never know how I love him; and that, not because he's handsome, Nelly, but because he's more myself than I am. Whatever our souls are made of, his and mine are the same, and Linton's is as different as a moonbeam from lightning, or frost from fire." Heathcliff, who has overheard her say it would degrade her to marry him, leaves the room and does not hear the final, the true, declaration. Yet whether he had heard it or not, he was correct in assuming that Catherine had betrayed their love because she was seduced by the offers the world makes to women to renounce their selves: adornment, "respect," protection, elegance, and the separation, except in giving birth, from the hardness of life.

Catherine, with such a love, chooses the conventional path, and the androgynous ideal achieves only a ghostly realization. Its only possible home being earth, this pair, who threw away their chance, must haunt the moors in eternal search for the ideal love, each in quest of the other half of himself which has been denied. For it is Cathy's masculine side which she has denied in marrying Linton and moving to Thrushcross Grange. Confined there, she sinks into death. "I'm wearying to escape into that glorious world, and to be always there; not seeing it dimly through tears, and yearning for it through the walls of an aching heart; but really with it, and in it. Nelly, you think you are better and more fortunate than I; in full health and strength. You are sorry for me—very soon that will be altered. I shall be sorry for *you.*" Nelly will still be in "this shattered prison" where Cathy is "tired of being enclosed." She has recognized that she will take Heathcliff with her into death because "he's in my soul."

Heathcliff's temptation, or inevitable fall into the anti-androgynous world, comes after Cathy's death, not before. The betrayal was hers, because of her sex and her background, and Heathcliff tells her so before she dies: "*Why* did you despise me? *Why* did you betray your own heart, Cathy? I have not one word of comfort. You deserve this. You have killed yourself. Yes, you may kiss me, and cry; and wring out my kisses and tears. They'll blight you—they'll damn you. You love me—then what *right* had you to leave me? What right—answer me—for the poor fancy you felt for Linton? Because misery, and degradation, and death, and nothing that God or Satan could inflict would have parted us, *you,* of your own will, did it. I have not broken your heart—*you* have broken it—and in breaking it, you have broken mine. So much the worse for me, that I am strong. Do I want to live? What kind of living will it be when you—oh, God! would *you* like to live with your soul in the grave?"

With his soul in the grave, Heathcliff follows the "masculine" pattern of self-expression. Devoted wholly to his own aggrandizement, whether in desire for revenge or in anger for deprivation, he treats his "wife," Linton's sister, in the manner of a cruel rake; he contrives to cheat and scheme to—as we would say today—make it. He grows rich and powerful. He uses the law to enrich himself, and deprive others. Utterly manly, he despises his "feminine" son, and tries to brutalize young Hareton. Heathcliff has followed the conventional pattern of his sex, into violence, brutality, and the feverish acquisition of wealth as Cathy had followed the conventional pattern of her sex into weakness, passivity, and luxury. They sank into their "proper sexual roles."

—Carolyn G. Heilbrun, "The Woman as Hero," *Toward a Recognition of Androgyny* (New York: Knopf, 1973), pp. 80–82

❖

[Terry Eagleton (b. 1943) is a Fellow of Wadham College, Oxford, and a leading British literary theorist. Among his many works are *Criticism and Ideology* (1976), *Literary Theory: An Introduction* (1983), and *Heathcliff and the Great Hunger: Studies in Irish Culture* (1995). In this extract, taken from his Marxist study of the Brontës, Eagleton asserts that Heathcliff is a disruptive force in the sociopolitical world of Wuthering Heights because he has no well-defined place in the economic system.]

Throughout *Wuthering Heights,* labour and culture, bondage and freedom, Nature and artifice appear at once as each other's dialectical negations and as subtly matched, mutually reflective. Culture—gentility—is the opposite of labour for young Heathcliff and Hareton; but it is also a crucial economic weapon, as well as a product of work itself. The delicate spiritless Lintons in their crimson-carpeted drawing-room are radically severed from the labour which sustains them; gentility grows from the production of others, detaches itself from that work (as the Grange is separate from the Heights), and then comes to dominate the labour on which it is parasitic. In doing so, it becomes a form of self-bondage; if work is servitude, so in a subtler sense is civilisation. To some extent, these polarities are held together in the yeoman-farming structure of the Heights. Here labour and culture, freedom and necessity, Nature and society are roughly complementary. The Earnshaws are gentlemen yet they work the land; they enjoy the freedom of being their own masters, but that freedom moves within the tough discipline of labour; and because the social unit of the Heights—the family—is both 'natural' (biological) and an economic system, it acts to some degree as a mediation between Nature and artifice, naturalising property relations and socialising blood-ties. Relationships in this isolated world are turbulently face-to-face, but they are also impersonally mediated through a working relation with Nature. This is not to share Mrs Q. D. Leavis's view of the Heights as 'a wholesome primitive and natural unit of a healthy society'; there does not, for instance, seem much that is wholesome about Joseph. Joseph incarnates a grimness inherent in conditions of economic exigency, where relationships must be tightly ordered and are easily warped into violence. One of *Wuthering Heights'* more notable achievements is ruthlessly to de-mystify the Victorian notion of the family as a pious, pacific space within social conflict. Even so, the Heights does pin together contradictions which the entry of Heathcliff will break open. Heathcliff disturbs the Heights because he is simply superfluous: he has no defined place within its biological and economic system. (He may well be Catherine's illegitimate half-brother, just as he may well have passed his two-year absence in Tunbridge Wells.) The superfluity he embodies is that of a sheerly human demand for recognition; but since there is no space for such surplus within the terse economy of the Heights, it proves destructive rather than creative in effect, straining and overloading already taut relationships. Heathcliff catalyses an aggression intrinsic to Heights society; that sound blow Hindley hands out to Catherine on the evening of Heathcliff's first appearance is slight but significant evidence against the case that conflict starts only with Heathcliff's arrival.

The effect of Heathcliff is to explode those conflicts into antagonisms which finally rip the place apart. In particular, he marks the beginnings of that process whereby passion and personal intensity separate out from the social domain and offer an alternative commitment to it. For farming families like the Earnshaws, work and human relations are roughly coterminous: work is socialised, personal relations mediated through a context of labour. Heathcliff, however, is set to work meaninglessly, as a servant rather than a member of the family; and his fervent emotional life with Catherine is thus forced outside the working environment into the wild Nature of the heath, rather than Nature reclaimed and worked up into significant value in the social activity of labour. Heathcliff is stripped of culture in the sense of gentility, but the result is a paradoxical intensifying of his fertile imaginative liaison with Catherine. It is fitting, then, that their free, neglected wanderings lead them to their adventure at Thrushcross Grange. For if the Romantic childhood culture of Catherine and Heathcliff exists in a social limbo divorced from the minatory world of working relations, the same can be said in a different sense of the genteel culture of the Lintons, surviving as it does on the basis of material conditions it simultaneously conceals. As the children spy on the Linton family, that concealed brutality is unleashed in the shape of bulldogs brought to the defence of civility. The natural energy in which the Lintons' culture is rooted bursts literally through to savage the 'savages' who appear to threaten property. The underlying truth of violence, continuously visible at the Heights, is momentarily exposed; old Linton thinks the intruders are after his rents. Culture draws a veil over such brute force but also sharpens it: the more property you have, the more ruthlessly you need to defend it. Indeed, Heathcliff himself seems dimly aware of how cultivation exacerbates 'natural' conflict, as we see in his scornful account of the Linton children's petulant squabbling; cultivation, by pampering and swaddling 'natural' drives, at once represses serious physical violence and breeds a neurasthenic sensitivity which allows selfish impulse free rein. 'Natural' aggression is nurtured both by an excess and an absence of culture—a paradox demonstrated by Catherine Earnshaw, who is at once wild and pettish, savage and spoilt. Nature and culture, then, are locked in a complex relation of antagonism and affinity: the Romantic fantasies of Heathcliff and Catherine, and the Romantic Linton drawing-room with its gold-bordered ceiling and shimmering chandelier, both bear the scars of the material conditions which produced them—scars visibly inscribed on Cathy's ankle. Yet to leave the matter there would be to draw a purely formal parallel. For what distinguishes the two forms of Romance is Heathcliff: his intense communion with Catherine is an uncompromising rejection of the Linton world.

—Terry Eagleton, *Myths of Power: A Marxist Study of the Brontës* (London: Macmillan Press, 1975), pp. 105–7

❖

PATRICIA MEYER SPACKS ON THE ADOLESCENCE OF CATHERINE

[Patricia Meyer Spacks (b. 1929), a professor of English at Wellesley College, is the author of many books of criticism, including *Imagining a Self: Autobiography and Novel in Eighteenth-Century England* (1976), *Desire and Truth: Functions of Plot in Eighteenth-Century English Novels* (1990), and *Boredom: The Literary History of a State of Mind* (1995). In this extract, Spacks argues that, although Heathcliff dominates much of the action of *Wuthering Heights,* it is Catherine's adolescent imagination that is victorious.]

Passion, that ambiguously valued state of feeling, dictates the plot of *Wuthering Heights,* itself an outpouring of a creative passion with some analogies to the less productive emotion that dominates Catherine and Heathcliff. The plot in its complexities keeps escaping the memory: one recalls the towering figure of Heathcliff, the desperate feelings of Catherine, but easily loses track of the intricacies through which the characters develop. Catherine and her brother Hindley, with their parents and their servants, Joseph and Nelly, inhabit the old house on the moor at Wuthering Heights. After Catherine's father brings home the mysterious foundling Heathcliff, the girl and the waif form an intense, rebellious alliance, weakened when Catherine makes friends with the prosperous and conventional Edgar Linton and his sister Isabella. Heathcliff, neglected and brutalized by Hindley after his father's death, disappears; Catherine marries Edgar; Hindley, whose young wife dies, sinks toward animality. When Heathcliff returns, he encourages Hindley's degradation. Catherine's deep attention still focuses on Heathcliff; Isabella promptly fancies herself in love with him. As part of his elaborate revenge on the Lintons and Hindley, Heathcliff marries Isabella, who soon flees his brutality but afterwards bears his son, Linton. Catherine dies in childbirth, leaving the infant Cathy, who as she grows becomes devoted to her father. After Isabella's death, Heathcliff reclaims his sickly, petulant son, and tricks Cathy into marrying Linton, imprisoning both at Wuthering Heights. Hindley has died; Edgar Linton soon follows him; Cathy's husband Linton dies shortly after her father, but Cathy remains Heathcliff's victim, as does Hindley's illiterate, degraded son, Hareton. Heathcliff's desire for victims weakens, however, as his obsession with the dead Catherine augments; he dies hoping for union with her, leaving Hareton and Cathy to redeem one another through mature love.

Such bare summary ignores the powerful effects achieved through disjunctive narrative and disparate points of view, particularly through the perspectives of the "outsider" Lockwood—narrator, spectator, and listener—and of self-righteous Nelly Dean. But it suggests the central issues of the novel. The grand passion that determines the fate of Catherine and Heathcliff is intense, diffuse (vaguely involving nature as well as individuals), and sterile. We may believe the lovers in their talk of some mystical union more powerful than death, but no earthly union results from their feeling. Their connection literally produces only destruction. Catherine's incompletely heard confession of her devotion to Heathcliff precipitates his exile, which hardens him into a machine organized for revenge. When Heathcliff returns, his initial appearance causes a quarrel between Catherine and her husband; a subsequent visit produces the painful scene of her articulated contempt for Edgar during which she locks the door and throws the key into the fire; conflict over Heathcliff provokes her desperate illness; his insistence on seeing her eventuates in her death. The side effects of this passion, equally disastrous, include the undoing of Isabella. Linton would never have been born were it not for Heathcliff's plotting; but this fertility contains the seeds of its own frustration. He is born only to be used by others, and to die. The survivors issue not from grand passions but from the union of Edgar and Catherine, Hindley and his socially inferior bride; they point toward the future.

But survival is not the highest of values, nor must the reader judge causes by their effects. Results may be irrelevant; or the truly significant results may be too subtle for evaluation. Catherine is, regardless of her death (perhaps partly *because* of it), a triumphant adolescent, her entire career a glorification of the undisciplined adolescent sensibility. Heathcliff, who looks so much more "manly" than Edgar, is as much as his soul mate an adolescent; more important, he is a projection of adolescent fantasy: give him a black leather jacket and a motorcycle and he'd fit right into many a youthful dream even now. Powerful, manly, mysterious, fully conscious of his own worth, frequently brutal, he remains nonetheless absolutely submissive to the woman he loves—if that is the proper verb. Around her he organizes his life. He provides her the opportunity for vicarious aggression, dominating her husband, tyrannizing over her conventional sister-in-law; when he turns his aggression toward her, though, she can readily master him. A powerful man controlled by a woman's power: when she dies, she draws him to her in death.

Heathcliff is partly a figment of Catherine's imagination as well as Emily Brontë's. Catherine's fantasies, far more daring than Emma's, are equally vital to her development. She focuses them on Heathcliff: if he were not there, she would have to invent him. In fact, she *does* invent him, directly and indirectly shaping his being. After his boyhood, he instigates no significant action that is not at least indirectly the result of his response to her. Because of her he goes away, returns, marries lovelessly, destroys Hindley, claims his own son as well as Hindley's, arranges Linton's marriage, finally dies. But Catherine is also controlled by her own creation, her important actions issuing from her bond to Heathcliff.

Although Heathcliff dominates the action of *Wuthering Heights,* and the imagination of its author and its other characters, Catherine more clearly exemplifies what the two of them stand for. Not yet nineteen when she dies, she cannot survive into maturity; Heathcliff, who lasts twice as long, matures hardly more. Both are transcendent narcissists. Catherine explains that she loves Heathcliff "because he's more myself than I am. Whatever our souls are made of, his and mine are the same, and [Edgar] Linton's is as different as a moonbeam from lightning, or frost from fire." Her analogies suggest the ground of her exalted self-esteem. She and Healthcliff share a fiery nature—a capacity for intense, dangerous feeling. The intensity and the danger are both criteria of value; by comparison the purity of the moonbeam, the clarity of frost seem negligible, even contemptible. Hot is better than cold: Catherine has no doubt about that. The heat of her sexuality and of her temper attest her superiority to the man she marries and her identity with the man she loves; her sense of self is the ground of all her values.

—Patricia Meyer Spacks, "The Adolescent as Heroine," *The Female Imagination* (New York: Knopf, 1975), pp. 136–38

❖

[Donald D. Stone (b. 1942) teaches at Queens College of the City University of New York. He is the coeditor of *Nineteenth-Century Lives: Essays Presented to Jerome Hamilton Buckley* (1989) and author of *The Romantic Impulse in Victorian Fiction* (1980), from which the following extract is taken. Here, Stone maintains that Brontë traverses the same "Byronic terrain" in *Wuthering Heights* later followed by Edward Bulwer-Lytton.]

Whether Emily Brontë intended her hero to be judged from the moral point of view that her sister applied to Rochester in *Jane Eyre* has never been resolved satisfactorily. Charlotte Brontë had no doubt about Heathcliff's "unredeemed" nature, but she suggested in her Preface to *Wuthering Heights* that Emily "did not know what she had done" when she created him, that her sister had acted under the force of a creative inspiration that had rendered her passive during the act of writing. No English novel has inspired such a diversity of interpretations as *Wuthering Heights;* and Heathcliff in particular has been viewed as an anarchic force of nature, a mythic figure thrust into the real world, a Byronic-derived Satanic outcast, a Marxist proletarian-rebel, a representation of the Freudian Id, and a reflection of the heroine's adolescent narcissism. One is tempted to suggest that the novel's popularity is in large part the result of its oblique allusions and its unwritten passages, those dealing, for example, with Heathcliff's origins or motivations, which later readers have interpreted or supplied themselves to suit their own interests. There is much to pity in Heathcliff's youthful deprivation; but as is the case with Bulwer's similarly bereft heroes, there is also something childish about his diabolical antics (such as hanging his wife Isabella's pet dog), something of the smell of Byronic greasepaint about his physiognomy ("A half-civilized ferocity lurked yet in the depressed brows and eyes, full of black fire"). A number of Victorian critics, in consequence, judged Heathcliff and his companions in the novel as representatives of "the brutalizing influence of unchecked passion . . . [,] a commentary on the truth that there is no tyranny in the world like that which thoughts of evil exercise in the daring and reckless breast" ⟨anonymous review in *Britannia*⟩. In this reading, Heathcliff is analogous to Bertha in *Jane Eyre:* not a hero, but a warning example of the self-destructiveness of the unregulated will. But where Charlotte Brontë deliberately put her characters into a moral context, her sister seems to have thought less in terms of conventional morality than of aesthetic logic—of the relations of her characters to literature rather than to life.

One is tempted to say that *Wuthering Heights* is the Bulwer-Lytton novel that Bulwer himself lacked the genius to write. It has many of Bulwer's stocks in trade: self-willed characters, supernatural occurrences, charged romantic landscapes, a love that transcends death. Within a Bulwer novel the description of Heathcliff's rage following Cathy's death would seem appropriate and properly absurd: "He dashed his head against the knotted trunk; and, lifting his eyes, howled, not like a man, but like a savage beast getting goaded to death with knives and spears." (One recalls the similarly thwarted Castruccio Cesarini's mad fits, in *Ernest Maltrevers,* or the desolation of Falkland after Lady Mandeville's death.) Emily Brontë's triumph was that she went over the same Byronic terrain—"a perfect misanthropist's heaven," as Lockwood describes it—as that followed by Bulwer, and yet avoided making her story seem like the stuff of parody. Bulwer's fiction proves that *Wuthering Heights* is not the great romantic exception among English novels, as was once thought to be the case; yet Emily Brontë had a sense of humor and a conviction that were denied Bulwer. However literary her characters may be in their origins, she believed in them sufficiently to make later readers accept their melodramatic rantings as the echoes of some primal force of reality.

—Donald D. Stone, *The Romantic Impulse in Victorian Fiction* (Cambridge, MA: Harvard University Press, 1980), pp. 42–43

❖

STEVIE DAVIES ON STRUCTURE AND POINT OF VIEW IN
WUTHERING HEIGHTS

[Stevie Davies is a British critic and author of *Emily
Brontë* (1988), *Milton* (1991), and *Emily Brontë:
Heretic* (1994). In this extract, taken from her earlier
book on Emily Brontë, Davies believes that the architecture of Catherine's bedroom is a parable of the conception of reality embodied by the novel.]

When the principal narrator of *Wuthering Heights,* Lockwood,
has to spend the night at the Heights, he is led in to a room
which in its turn contains a smaller room. This is the clothes-
press in which the elder Catherine had slept as a child. To get
in, he has to slide away the side-panel. Inside this womb- or
tomb-like place, he finds a window, upon whose ledge are a
few old, mildewed books, and the three scratched names—
Catherine Earnshaw, Catherine Heathcliff, Catherine Linton.
Lockwood is a constitutional voyeur; he cannot help climbing
in and peering round at other people's business. In telling the
story, he provides the framed window of his mind in order that
we too can scrutinize certain secret places. Lockwood himself
is glad of the privacy of the press, feeling 'secure against the
vigilance of Heathcliff, and everyone else'. This is not surprising
in view of the fact that, in attempting a getaway from the
unwelcoming inhabitants of the Heights, he has just been set
on by 'two hairy monsters' named as the dogs Gnasher and
Wolf, causing him to emit an outburst of choice and unexpected oaths, and an undignified nose-bleed, to the amusement of
his host. Lockwood feels so sorely ill-used that he is able to
compare himself in his sufferings with no less a person than
King Lear on the heath.

The architecture of the dead Catherine's bedroom, with its
window-within-a-room-within-a-room, and Lockwood peering
about inside, is like a parable of the conception of reality which
the novel enacts. Reality for Emily Brontë is intricately relativis-
tic. She raises the familiar premise that life is a mesh of anecdotes, which can be related on the 'I said to her and she said to
me' principle, to the status of a philosophical system. The
author never tells you what to think, or how to interpret the

material which comes filtered through so many people's inset dreams, anecdotes, letters, hieroglyphs, diaries, snatches of song, reminiscences, inscriptions on houses and signposts. You have to draw deductions as you do in life itself, whose riddles and clues no authority can conclusively solve, and it is just to be hoped that you will be a little less idiotic than Lockwood, rather less sententious than Nelly, in coming to your conclusions. *Wuthering Heights* rudely mocks its reader. Equally it haunts her or him. Like the bits of diary which Lockwood is able to decipher in the press, Emily Brontë does not offer her book as a fictitious means of bridging the gap between present and past: she reclaims only fragments, leaving us to guess or dream the rest, so that we feel the presence of the elder Catherine's childhood and of her survival after death with the most vivid certainty, yet are not given the slightest conclusive evidence for that survival. Lockwood as a 'reader' of these experiences is not so different from ourselves reading and trying to make sense of the fragments he pieces together, despite the fact that we are encouraged to laugh at him. With his vision framed by his own inadequacies, which are legion, Lockwood (trying to get further and further in to the true story of the Heights) only has access to a framed reality, and cannot know what to call interior, and what exterior—appearance or reality—since every 'inside' place seems to enclose and therefore be displaced upsettingly by yet another 'inside'. For within the closet are books. Inside the books is the elder Catherine's fragmentary diary, scrawled down the margins of the New Testament. This is Catherine's own testament, like a window into the past through which we can glimpse only odd views and catch scraps of conversation (as in Emily's and Anne's own diary-papers). Worryingly, there seem to be three Catherines, each with a different surname: the 'characters'—a fruitful pun suggesting both individuals and handwriting—are baffling, and seem maliciously capable of raising spectres, for when Lockwood nods off the air seems to swarm with Catherines, and he jerks hurriedly awake. By the end of the novel we have solved the riddle of the three Catherines, Earnshaw marrying Linton, begetting a Linton who will marry a Heathcliff, but by the end we have travelled on to a last and first Catherine: the younger Cathy who in a new testament returns to the old in marrying an Earnshaw. The cycle is riddling and confusing, even when we know the answer.

—Stevie Davies, *Emily Brontë: The Artist as a Free Woman* (Manchester, UK: Carcanet Press, 1983), pp. 114–15

❖

U. C. KNOEPFLMACHER ON THE CREATION OF HEATHCLIFF

[U. C. Knoepflmacher (b. 1931), a professor of English at Princeton University, is the author of *Religious Humanism and the Victorian Novel* (1965), *George Eliot's Early Novels* (1968), and *Nature and the Victorian Imagination* (1977). In this extract from his study of *Wuthering Heights,* Knoepflmacher asserts that, like Mary Shelley's Frankenstein, Heathcliff is a creation partly of flesh and blood and partly of desire.]

Who and *what* is Heathcliff? The question is asked by both Nelly and Isabella. Although Heathcliff is a character in his own right, he is as much the product of animated desire as that nameless sufferer from gender-bifurcations, the Frankenstein Monster. Shelley's creature, fashioned from the tissue of dead men (and women?), is an "it" until converted to male sadism. The boy whom old Earnshaw presents as an "it" is so denominated by Nelly no less than seventeen times until "he" is christened with a dead infant's name that "has served *him* ever since" (ch. 4). "Heathcliff" (the very name, like "Frankenstein," combining openness with hardness) thus exists, I would contend, essentially as part of a relation, first between child/parent and then, more intensely, of boy/girl selves. He is a metaphor made literal, enfleshed. Shaped by a world in which children must grow up and assume rigid identities, he feels betrayed. Only by returning into the metaphoric realm of essences into which Catherine precedes him can he confirm her credo: "I cannot express it," she had told Nelly; "but surely you and everybody have a notion that there is, or should be, an existence beyond you" (ch. 9). It seems hard not to hear Emily

Brontë's own accents in this and similar utterances by Catherine and Heathcliff. For *Wuthering Heights* registers, among other things, her disagreement with the two sisters who had come to accept their containment in a reality like Nelly Dean's.

What, then, is Heathcliff/Catherine? Their fusion, separation, and reintegration is cast through the form of kinship most frequently found in this novel of repetitions and redoublings, that of a brother and a sister. There are no less than six brother/sister pairs if we include cousins and foster-siblings:

literal	*metaphoric*	*literal/metaphoric:*
Hindley/Catherine	CATHERINE/HEATHCLIFF	Linton Heathcliff/Cathy
Edgar/Isabella	Nelly/Hindley	HARETON/CATHY

A seventh pair might be added to the other six in the shape of Nelly and Heathcliff. Whether or not these two outsiders are actually Old Earnshaw's illegitimate children is irrelevant. As Hindley's foster-sister and Catherine's foster-brother, the novel's main opponents automatically become each other's foster-siblings.

We have noted that the Hareton/Cathy marriage with which the "Earnshaw Chronicle" ends condenses Catherine's relations to her two "brothers," Heathcliff and Hindley; the union between Nelly's prime nursling and her foster-brother's son also produces a consummation, once removed, between Nelly and Hindley. Edgar and Isabella, that other alienated pair of siblings, can be said to "marry" each other through the brief union of their children, when Cathy becomes Linton Heathcliff's bride, in what can also be considered as still another surrogate espousal between Heathcliff and Catherine. The permutations of this central metaphor of fusing and diffusing brother/sister selves so overwhelm us by their variety that we give our relieved assent to the final contractions of Cathy/Hareton and Catherine/Heathcliff.

If, as I have been suggesting, Emily Brontë's fable of childhood lost and regained stems from her desire to reassert the violated imaginative oneness she once shared with her siblings, it seems unclear at first why she would not have chosen to portray her four children, as her sister Charlotte did in *Jane Eyre,* as three sisters and one brother. In her own tale about a disempowered Cinderella, Charlotte twice situates Jane into a domestic foursome. As a child, Jane is rejected by her Reed cousins, Eliza, Georgiana, and John, the offspring of her mother's brother; as an adult, however she is welcomed by her Rivers cousins, Diana, Mary, and St. John, the children of her father's sister. Both the grotesque John Reed and the handsome St. John are unacceptable as sexual partners. For, unlike Cathy (who finds happiness through Hareton), Jane must wed someone who is not a blood relation. The taint of incest that in some societies still attaches to the marriage of cousins thus can be safely avoided. Charlotte, after all, wants to invest Jane with social, rather than primitive or asocial, powers. Emily, on the other hand, invests Heathcliff's abdication of all power with the same intense pleasure Jane experiences after she gains control over her maimed lover. Jane's erotic passion for Rochester, sanctioned only after his crippling, manifests itself in Emily's novel only when Heathcliff becomes free to make love to a sisterly ghost. In this sense, *Wuthering Heights* and *Jane Eyre* are affirmations of exactly contrary realities.

—U. C. Knoepflmacher, *Emily Brontë:* Wuthering Heights (Cambridge: Cambridge University Press, 1989), pp. 96–98

❖

ROBERT M. POLHEMUS ON LOVE AND DEATH IN *WUTHERING HEIGHTS*

[Robert M. Polhemus, a professor of English at Stanford University, is the author of *The Changing World of Anthony Trollope* (1968), *Comic Faith: The Great Comic Tradition from Austen to Joyce* (1980), and *Erotic Faith: Being in Love from Jane Austen to D. H. Lawrence* (1990), from which the following extract is taken. Here, Polhemus notes the prevalence of death in *Wuthering Heights* and believes that the characters attempt to defeat it by love or eroticism.]

What happens to you after you die? Many people find that religious faith helps them face that question without falling into despair. Desire for transcendence, not just of the self but of the self's mortality, has motivated the will to faith since the first syllable of recorded time; and, if love is a faith, we ought to find that some of its devotees see it as a hope in confronting— or avoiding—the problem of personal death and annihilated consciousness. Death haunts Emily Brontë's *Wuthering Heights,* as it so terribly haunted the Brontë family, and in its pages she imagines a mystical, passionate calling as a way of facing the immanent and imminent mortal agony. The book, as earthy a piece of Victorian fiction as there is, grounds grand romantic passion in the gross texture of everyday life. Nevertheless, it is a crucial text of mystical erotic vocation, raising and forcing most of the critical issues that swirl about romantic love in the post-Renaissance era.

Emily Brontë's characters talk repeatedly about afterlife. No novelist's imagination has ever bound love and death more closely together, and no nineteenth-century writer more clearly shows the relation between the menace of unredeemed, meaningless death and the rise of popular faith in romantic love. Hating and fearing death, people have often professed to welcome it as a release into eternal joy. If you are good, you may go to heaven when you die; you may find "peace." Some form of that idea has been a traditional solace of religion. In one of her famous speeches, Catherine Earnshaw, to the chagrin of conventional Nelly Dean, rejects such orthodoxy. "If I were in heaven, Nelly, I should be extremely miserable. . . . I dreamt, once, that I was there. . . . heaven did not seem to be my home; and I broke my heart with weeping to come back to earth; and the angels were so angry that they flung me out, into the middle of the heath on the top of Wuthering Heights; . . . That will do to explain my secret." It will do also to explain the novel's title: "Wuthering Heights" means the rejection of heaven. Reject heaven and you reject angels—even angels-in-the-house. We have here the complaint of romantic individualism that Christian heaven—theocratic authority called bliss and made perpetual—does not seem to be an inviting place or a satisfactory consolation for death.

But it is one thing for advanced poets like Blake, Byron, and Shelley to side with Satan's rebellion against heaven, and another for a Yorkshire parson's daughter to find the dogma of afterlife wanting. We are confronting a growing crisis for orthodox faith. *Wuthering Heights* is filled with a religious urgency—unprecedented in British novels—to imagine a faith that might replace the old. Cathy's "secret" is blasphemous, and Emily Brontë's secret, in the novel, is the raging heresy that has become common in modern life: redemption, if it is possible, lies in personal desire, imaginative power, and love. Nobody else's heaven is good enough. Echoing Cathy, Heathcliff says late in the book, "I have nearly attained *my* heaven; and that of others is altogether unvalued and uncoveted by me!" Even Cathy II and young Linton imagine their own ideas of the perfect heaven. The hope for salvation becomes a matter of eroticized private enterprise.

Faith tries to reconcile what, to reason, is irreconcilable. Consciousness of death and of the self defines us as human, and yet human beings try to deny the death of the self. Catherine and Heathcliff have faith in their vocation of being in love with one another. Says she, "If all else perished, and *he* remained, I should still continue to be; and, if all else remained, and he were annihilated, the Universe would turn to a mighty stranger. I should not seem a part of it." He cries that "nothing"—not "death," not "God or Satan"—has the strength to part them. They both believe that they have their being in the other, as Christians, Jews, and Moslems believe that they have their being in God. Look at the mystical passion of these two: devotion to shared experience and intimacy with the other; willingness to suffer anything, up to, and including, death, for the sake of this connection; ecstatic expression; mutilation of both social custom and the flesh; and mania for self-transcendence through the other. That passion is a way of overcoming the threat of death and the separateness of existence. Their calling is to *be* the other; and that calling, mad and destructive as it sometimes seems, is religious.

Wuthering Heights features the desire to transgress normal limitations, and that desire accounts for its violence and for the eccentric, fascinating flow of libido in it. If we think of the three major acts and areas of erotic transgression for the nineteenth-century imagination—sadism, incest, and adultery—and then consider how the Cathy-Heathcliff love story touches on them, we can see why the novel has had such a mind-jangling effect. It's a very kinky book, replete with polymorphous perversity, sadomasochism, necrophilia, hints of pedophilia, and even a bent towards polyandry, as well as incest and adultery. All this, however, figures in the urge to free the spirit from social conventions, the world, and the galling limitation of the body. That dispersed eroticism, shocking as it is, connects with an underlying drive for the breaking of boundaries—transgression as a means to transcendence.

> —Robert M. Polhemus, "The Passionate Calling: Emily Brontë's *Wuthering Heights* (1847)," *Erotic Faith: Being in Love from Jane Austen to D. H. Lawrence* (Chicago: University of Chicago Press, 1990), pp. 81–83

❖

SHEILA SMITH ON SUPERNATURALISM AND BALLADRY IN *WUTHERING HEIGHTS*

[Sheila Smith is a Canadian literary scholar. In this extract, she believes that the supernaturalism in *Wuthering Heights* is derived from Brontë's familiarity with traditional ballads, whose paganism and emphasis on passion are reflected in the novel.]

The ballads are fundamentally important to *Wuthering Heights,* especially to the novel's version of the supernatural which records the chief characters' triumphant attainment of a spiritual life, bringing them into accord with each other and with Nature. This life transcends the restrictions of contemporary class prejudices, evades the law (Heathcliff is both metaphorically and, by his cunning, literally outside the scope of the law and with which Nelly threatens him) and disregards orthodox morality, so often used as an instrument of oppression. Wimberly emphasizes the pagan nature of the ballads: 'The remains of heathendom in folksong are especially marked . . . the ideas and practices imbedded in British balladry may be referred almost wholly to a pagan culture.' In the novel the pagan world, centred on sexual passion, expressed in the supernatural tale of Heathcliff and Cathy's enduring love, is constantly set against orthodox Christianity, of the routine kind dutifully voiced by Nelly or referred to by Lockwood or Edgar Linton; or the more lurid morality of Calvinistic sects such as Joseph's. Ironically, Joseph, who is constantly inveighing against the pleasures of this life and insisting on the demands of the next, does not convince the reader that he is possessed of the life of the spirit. Joseph's religion is a brand of individualistic materialism, insisting on the return which his outlay of good conduct will ensure him. Despite his continual and vehement references to the Devil, Joseph is not in contact with the supernatural. He remains simply a cantankerous old man, using the terms of his religion to vent his spite against youth, vigour, and love.

In *Wuthering Heights* Emily Brontë revitalizes the literary form of the novel by use of structural devices, motifs, and subjects which properly belong to the oral tradition with which all the Brontë children were familiar, particularly through the agency of Tabitha Aykroyd, the Yorkshire woman who for thirty years was servant in the Brontë household. Elizabeth Gaskell, in her biography of Charlotte, says of Tabby that 'she had known the "bottom", or valley, in those primitive days when the fairies frequented the margin of the "beck" on moonlight nights, and had known folk who had seen them'. ⟨. . .⟩

By adapting in one of the newer genres of the literature of high culture elements of one of the older forms of the literature of folk culture, Emily Brontë extends and develops both Wordsworth's perception of imagination playing upon the familiar to give insight into the human condition, and Coleridge's apprehension of the supernatural as familiar. In *Wuthering Heights* imagination, in the supernatural manifestations, *is* insight, as against the cloudy perceptions of reason and orthodox morality. Her version of reality challenges the materialistic, class-ridden structure of the society of 1847, as Arnold Kettle and Terry Eagleton have suggested. But as Q. D. Leavis maintains that the allusions to fairy-tales in the novel are a sign of immaturity, so Eagleton argues that the supernatural is a weakness in the book, that Emily Brontë makes a 'metaphysical' challenge to society, but can do this 'only by refracting it through the distorting terms of existing social relations, while simultaneously, at a "deeper" level, isolating that challenge in a realm eternally divorced from the actual'. But, as I have tried to show, the novel's power lies in Emily Brontë's perception of the supernatural as an essential dimension of the actual, and this theme, central in ballad and folk-tale, is expressed by techniques which can be related to those of ballad and folk-tale. She uses the supernatural in her narrative to give direct, dramatic, and objective expression to the strength of sexual passion, as so many of the ballads do. It was this directness which so shocked Emily Brontë's first readers. 'Coarseness' and lack of orthodox morality were charges frequently levelled against the book. Even the perceptive G. H. Lewes, who could not 'deny its truth', found it also 'rude' and 'brutal'. The more obtuse E. P. Whipple, although he acknowledged 'Acton Bell's' (*sic*) 'uncommon talents', objected to 'his subject and his dogged manner of handling it'. Miriam Allott comments that it was Whipple who regarded *Wuthering Heights* 'as the last desperate attempt to corrupt the virtues of the sturdy descendants of the Puritans'. It was left to Swinburne, who had himself been ostracized for setting his poetry against the bourgeois morality of High Victorian society, to make the most perceptive comment on the novel: 'All the works of the elder sister [Charlotte Brontë] are rich in poetic spirit, poetic feeling, and poetic detail; but the younger sister's work is essentially and definitely a poem in the fullest and most positive sense of the term.' For 'poem' read 'ballad'.

—Sheila Smith, " 'At Once Strong and Eerie': The Supernatural in *Wuthering Heights* and Its Debt to the Traditional Ballad," *Review of English Studies* No. 172 (November 1992): 515–17

❖

Works by Emily Brontë

Poems by Currer, Ellis, and Acton Bell (with Charlotte and Anne Brontë). 1846.

Wuthering Heights. 1847. 2 vols.

Wuthering Heights and Agnes Grey ⟨by Anne Brontë⟩, *with a Biographical Notice of the Authors, a Selection from Their Literary Remains, and a Preface by Currer Bell* ⟨Charlotte Brontë⟩. 1850.

The Life and Works of Charlotte Brontë and Her Sisters. 1872–73. 7 vols.

The Works of Charlotte, Emily, and Anne Brontë. Ed. F. J. S. 1893. 12 vols.

The Life and Works of the Sisters Brontë. Ed. Mrs. Humphry Ward and Clement K. Shorter. 1899–1903. 7 vols.

The Novels and Poems of Charlotte, Emily, and Anne Brontë. 1901–07. 7 vols.

The Works of Charlotte, Emily, and Anne Brontë. Ed. Temple Scott. 1901. 12 vols.

Poems by Charlotte, Emily, and Anne Brontë. 1902.

Poems. Ed. Arthur Symons. 1906.

The Brontës: Life and Letters. Ed. Clement K. Shorter. 1908. 2 vols.

Complete Works. Ed. Clement K. Shorter and W. Robertson Nicoll. 1910–11. 2 vols.

Complete Poems. Ed. Clement K. Shorter and C. W. Hatfield. 1923.

The Shakespeare Head Brontë (with Charlotte and Emily Brontë). Ed. Thomas J. Wise and John Alexander Symington. 1931–38. 19 vols.

The Brontës: Their Lives, Friendships, and Correspondence.
Ed. Thomas J. Wise and John Alexander Symington. 1932.
4 vols.

Two Poems: Love's Rebuke, Remembrance. Ed. Fanny E.
Ratchford. 1934.

*Gondal Poems: Now First Published from the MS. in the British
Museum.* Ed. Helen Brown and Joan Mott. 1938.

Complete Poems. Ed. C. W. Hatfield. 1941.

Five Essays Written in French. Tr. Lorrine W. Nagel. Ed. Fanny E.
Ratchford. 1948.

Complete Poems. Ed. Philip Henderson. 1951.

A Selection of Poems. Ed. Muriel Spark. 1952.

Gondal's Queen: A Novel in Verse. Ed. Fanny E. Ratchford.
1955.

Poems. Ed. Rosemary Harthill. 1973.

The Novels of Charlotte, Emily, and Anne Brontë. Ed. Hilda
Marsden, Ian Jack et al. 1976– .

Selected Poems (with Anne and Charlotte Brontë). Ed. Tom
Winnifrith and Edward Chitham. 1985.

The Brontës: Selected Poems. Ed. Juliet R. Barker. 1985.

Poems. Ed. Barbara Lloyd-Evans. 1992.

The Complete Poems. Ed. Janet Gezari. 1992.

Works about Emily Brontë and Wuthering Heights

Allott, Miriam, ed. Wuthering Heights: *A Casebook.* London: Macmillan, 1970.

Barreca, Regina. "The Power of Excommunication: Sex and the Feminine Text in *Wuthering Heights.*" In *Sex and Death in Victorian Literature,* ed. Regina Barreca. London: Macmillan, 1990, pp. 227–40.

Benvenuto, Richard. *Emily Brontë.* Boston: Twayne, 1982.

Berman, Jeffrey. "Attachment and Loss in *Wuthering Heights.*" In Berman's *Narcissism and the Novel.* New York: New York University Press, 1990, pp. 78–112.

Bloom, Harold, ed. *The Brontës.* New York: Chelsea House, 1986.

———, ed. *Emily Brontë's* Wuthering Heights. New York: Chelsea House, 1987.

———, ed. *Heathcliff.* New York: Chelsea House, 1993.

Chitham, Edward. *The Brontës' Irish Background.* New York: St. Martin's Press, 1986.

———. *A Life of Emily Brontë.* Oxford: Basil Blackwell, 1987.

Clayton, Jay. "*Wuthering Heights.*" In Clayton's *Romantic Vision and the Novel.* Cambridge: Cambridge University Press, 1987, pp. 81–102.

Daleski, H. M. "*Wuthering Heights:* The Whirl of Contraries." In Daleski's *The Divided Heroine: A Recurrent Pattern in Six English Novels.* New York: Holmes & Meier, 1984, pp. 25–46.

Davies, Stevie. *Emily Brontë.* Bloomington: Indiana University Press, 1988.

———. *Emily Brontë, Heretic.* London: Women's Press, 1994.

DeLamotte, Eugenia C. "Boundaries of the Self as Romantic Theme: Emily Brontë." In DeLamotte's *Perils of the Night: A Feminist Study of Nineteenth-Century Female Gothic.* New York: Oxford University Press, 1990, pp. 118–43.

Duthie, Enid L. *The Brontës and Nature.* New York: St. Martin's Press, 1986.

Frank, Katherine. *A Chainless Soul: A Life of Emily Brontë.* Boston: Houghton Mifflin, 1990.

Gérin, Winifred. *Emily Brontë: A Biography.* Oxford: Clarendon Press, 1971.

Ghnassia, Jill Dix. *Metaphysical Rebellion in the Works of Emily Brontë: A Reinterpretation.* New York: St. Martin's Press, 1994.

Gilbert, Sandra M., and Susan Gubar. "Looking Oppositely: Emily Brontë's Bible of Hell." In Gilbert and Gubar's *The Madwoman in the Attic: The Woman Writer and the Nineteenth-Century Literary Imagination.* New Haven: Yale University Press, 1979, pp. 248–308.

Goff, Barbara Munson. "Between Natural Theology and Natural Selection: Breeding the Human Animal in *Wuthering Heights.*" *Victorian Studies* 27 (1983–84): 477–508.

Heywood, Christopher. "A Yorkshire Background for *Wuthering Heights.*" *Modern Language Review* 88 (1993): 817–30.

Homans, Margaret. "The Name of the Mother in *Wuthering Heights.*" In *Bearing the Word: Language and Female Experience in Nineteenth-Century Women's Writing.* Chicago: University of Chicago Press, 1986, pp. 68–83.

Jacobs, Carol. *Uncontrollable Romanticism: Shelley, Brontë, Kleist.* Baltimore: Johns Hopkins University Press, 1989.

Kermode, Frank. "A Modern Way with a Classic." *New Literary History* 5 (1973–74): 415–34.

Knapp, Bettina L. *The Brontës: Branwell, Anne, Emily, Charlotte.* New York: Continuum, 1991.

Liddell, Robert. *Twin Spirits: The Novels of Emily and Anne Brontë.* London: Peter Owen, 1990.

Miller, J. Hillis. "*Wuthering Heights:* Repetition and the 'Uncanny.'" In Miller's *Fiction and Repetition.* Cambridge, MA: Harvard University Press, 1982, pp. 42–72.

Newman, Beth. " 'The Situation of the Looker-On': Gender, Narration, and Gaze in *Wuthering Heights.*" *PMLA* 105 (1990): 1029–41.

Oates, Joyce Carol. "The Magnanimity of *Wuthering Heights.*" *Critical Inquiry* 9 (1982): 435–49.

Paglia, Camille. "Romantic Shadows: Emily Brontë." In Paglia's *Sexual Personae: Art and Decadence from Nefertiti to Emily Dickinson.* New Haven: Yale University Press, 1990, pp. 439–59.

Pratt, Linda Ray. "'I Shall Be Your Father': Heathcliff's Narrative of Paternity." *Victorians Institute Journal* 20 (1992): 13–38.

Pykett, Lyn. *Emily Brontë.* Savage, MD: Barnes & Noble, 1989.

Smith, Anne, ed. *The Art of Emily Brontë.* London: Vision Press; Totowa, NJ: Barnes & Noble, 1976.

Spark, Muriel, and Derek Stanford. *Emily Brontë: Her Life and Work.* New York: Coward-McCann, 1966.

Stevenson, W. H. "*Wuthering Heights:* The Facts." *Essays in Criticism* 35 (1985): 149–66.

Tayler, Irene. *Holy Ghosts: The Male Muses of Emily and Charlotte Brontë.* New York: Columbia University Press, 1990.

Thomas, Ronald R. "Dreams and Disorders in *Wuthering Heights.*" In Thomas's *Dreams of Authority: Freud and the Fictions of the Unconscious.* Ithaca, NY: Cornell University Press, 1990, pp. 112–35.

Visick, Mary. *The Genesis of* Wuthering Heights. 3rd ed. Gloucester, UK: Ian Hodgkins, 1980.

Wallace, Robert K. *Emily Brontë and Beethoven.* Athens: University of Georgia Press, 1986.

Williams, Meg Harris. *A Strange Way of Killing: The Poetic Structure of* Wuthering Heights. Strathtay, UK: Clunie Press, 1987.

Winnifrith, Tom. *The Brontës and Their Background: Romance and Reality.* London: Macmillan, 1973.

Index of
Themes and Ideas

AUSTEN, JANE, as compared to Emily Brontë, 40

BELL, ACTON. *See* BRONTE, EMILY

BERTHA (*Jane Eyre*), as compared to Heathcliff, 62

BRONTE, ANNE, 8; as compared to Emily Brontë, 64

BRONTE, CHARLOTTE, 8; as compared to Emily Brontë, 35, 36, 37, 61, 62, 66–67, 71, 72; criticism of *Wuthering Heights,* 29–32

BRONTE, EMILY: heroines in her works, 36–37; life of, 8–9

DEAN, NELLY, and her role in the novel, 10, 12, 13, 14, 15, 16, 17, 18, 19, 20, 21, 22–23, 28, 31, 34, 41, 47, 50, 51, 52, 53, 54, 58, 59, 65, 66, 68, 70, 71

EARNSHAW, CATHERINE (CATHY): and her adolescence, 57–60; and her role in the novel, 10, 11, 12, 13, 14, 15, 16, 17, 19, 20, 22, 23, 24, 27, 28, 30, 34, 36, 37, 38, 39, 44, 45, 46, 47, 48, 49, 50, 51, 53, 54, 56, 62, 63, 64, 65, 66, 68, 69, 70, 71

EARNSHAW, HARETON, and his role in the novel, 10, 13, 14, 15, 16, 17, 18, 19, 20, 21, 24, 38, 45, 49, 50, 51, 54, 55, 58, 60, 66, 67

EARNSHAW, HINDLEY, and his role in the novel, 11, 12, 13, 14, 16, 17, 18, 22, 23–24, 34, 36, 38, 44, 45, 56, 58, 59, 60, 66

EYRE, JANE (*Jane Eyre*), as compared to Catherine Earnshaw, 28, 36, 37, 66–67

FAULKNER, WILLIAM, as compared to Emily Brontë, 52

GLENARVON (Lamb), and how it compares, 35

HEATHCLIFF: creation of, 65–67; as archetypal demon, 25–26, 42–44; and his diction, 51–52; and his revenge, 38–39; and his role in the novel, 10, 11, 12, 13, 14, 15, 16, 17, 18, 19, 20, 22, 23, 24, 27, 28, 30, 32, 34, 36, 37, 40, 49, 50, 53, 55, 56, 57, 58, 59, 60, 61, 62, 63, 69, 70, 71; his sadism, 45–48

HEATHCLIFF, LINTON, and his role in the novel, 17, 18, 19, 23, 24, 34, 37, 38, 39, 45, 53, 58, 60, 64, 66, 69

HUGO, VICTOR, as compared to Emily Brontë, 33, 35

JAMES, HENRY, as compared to Emily Brontë, 41

JANE EYRE (C. Brontë), and how it compares, 25, 27, 35, 61, 62, 66–67

JOSEPH, and his role in the novel, 10, 11, 16, 28, 31, 50, 56, 58, 71

LINTON, CATHERINE, and her role in the novel, 17, 18, 19, 20, 21, 23, 24, 28, 31, 34, 37, 38, 45, 49, 50, 53, 58, 66, 67, 69

LINTON, EDGAR, and his role in the novel, 12, 13, 14, 15, 16, 17, 18, 22, 23, 24, 27, 31, 34, 38, 39, 49, 53, 54, 55, 58, 59, 60, 66, 71

LINTON, ISABELLA, and her role in the novel, 12, 13, 14, 15, 16, 17, 22, 23, 24, 34, 37, 38, 39, 45, 54, 55, 58, 61, 65, 66

LOCKWOOD, MR., and his role in the novel, 10, 11, 14, 16, 20, 22, 23, 34, 37, 40, 44, 50, 51, 52, 59, 62, 63, 64, 71

NATURE, as theme, 14, 16, 30, 32, 40–42, 50, 55, 56, 61–62, 69

ROCHESTER (Jane Eyre), as compared to Heathcliff, 36, 61

SAND, GEORGE, as compared to Emily Brontë, 34, 35

SHIRLEY (C. Brontë), and how it compares to, 35

VILLETTE (C. Brontë), and how it compares to, 35

WUTHERING HEIGHTS: androgyny in, 52–54; Charlotte Brontë's criticism of, 29–32; central characters of, 26–29; depravity of, 25–26; economics and politics in, 55–57; emotional chaos in, 39–40; love and death in, 67–70; unity with nature in, 40–42; purity of passion in, 32–33; romantic elements in, 33–35; romantic setting of, 61–62; structure and point of view in, 63–65; supernaturalism and balladry in, 70–73; thematic and structural analysis of, 10–21; Thrushcross Grange and Wuthering Heights in, 48–50